Entertaining
God
and Influencing Cities

Entertaining God
and Influencing Cities

P. Douglas Small

Alive Publications • Kannapolis, NC

Book Editor: Wanda Griffith
Editorial Assistant: Tammy Hatfield
Copy Editors: Jessica Tressler
Esther Metaxas

Library of Congress Catalog Card Number: 2007921632

ISBN: 978-0-9820115-0-8

Copyright © 2008 by P. Douglas Small
Published by Alive Publications,
PO Box 1245, Kannapolis, NC 28082
in association with Project Pray
www.projectpray.org

Dedication

This book is dedicated to Barbara Ruth,
my wife for 40 years.

She has taught me how to live
in the presence of God.
No one else I know so easily
communes with God,
cares for others, and
loves so unconditionally.

Thanks, Barbara, for loving the Lord so much . . .
for five children, thirteen grandchildren,
and a wonderful life.

Contents

Introduction

D r. Lee was one of the most popular professors at the school, but he was not an advocate of prayer. Each year, during the Thanksgiving
season, he would offer an anti-prayer demon-
stration in his first-year chemistry class.
Holding up a glass goblet that he intended to
drop, he would challenge any prayer-believ-
ing student in the class to stand and ask God
to prevent the glass from breaking when it collided with the hard surface of the floor. For 12
years, the challenge went unanswered. For 12
years, young Christians left that classroom
intimidated. It was a kind of conditioning for
young believers—"If you believe in prayer at
this place, you'd better stay quiet about it in
Dr. Lee's class!"

The whole world seems bent on conditioning
us to stay quiet, to keep faith private, to force
prayer into the recesses of culture, to shout unbelief so loudly it would drown out believing
voices. The evidence against God is lined up in
such a rationally convincing way that even people with sound faith tremble. Society creates
systems that prevent evidence from being presented that would dash the cynical rationalism
of our time.

Year after year, students left the classroom
of Dr. Lee intimidated into silence. It was a kind
of intellectual persecution! "You surely don't

believe in prayer? In God? Not anymore? Not any of you? If you do, speak now or forever hold your peace!"

Such challenges are presumptuous. They are tempting God. It is what Lucifer suggested to Jesus: "Leap from the pinnacle of the Temple and force the hand of God to provide supernatural protection!" (See Matthew 4:5-7). We will gain little by entering into such trivial contests offered by the world. God is no circus performer. He will not show up to do an act. And yet, there are moments when He chooses to disclose Himself, to say to skeptics, "I am alive." Such moments become doorways into faith. Some will believe; others may doubt.

That morning, a young student answered Dr. Lee's challenge. He stood and offered to pray. With a mix of sarcasm and sensitivity, the professor offered to postpone the showdown. The experience could wait until after the holiday, and the student could arrange to have his pastor or others present for support. He declined.

He prayed a simple prayer: "God, I know that You can hear me. Please honor the name of Your Son, Jesus Christ, and honor me, Your servant. Don't let the flask break. Amen."

It was an uncomplicated prayer; precise; one focused on the honor of God. Dr. Lee extended his hand, holding out the glass flask. He opened his hand and let it fall. All in the room would witness something strange. No one could suggest a natural cause. There was no wind, no open windows, no irregular movement. And yet the glass fell, not downward in a straight, vertical path, but it fell at a decided angle. It hit the toe of Dr. Lee's shoe and then innocently rolled onto the floor unbroken.[1]

It was as if David had slain Goliath. Students whistled and cheered. They clapped and shouted. They stood to their feet and applauded. The muzzle was off. The season of intimidation was over. Dr. Lee ended his annual lectures against prayer. Someone had entertained God. And God had mysteriously shown up in a way that no one could have predicted.

---

[1] Richard Harvey, *Seventy Years of Miracles* (Camp Hill, PA: Horizon House, 1998), 64-65.

An Overview of Genesis 18

When God Comes, History Finds New Direction!
What kind of God would reveal Himself to a simple shepherd like Abraham? And therefore to simple folks like you and me? What kind of God would drop in for personal visits? Whisper His secrets to a wanderer? Immortalize Him? And, "Who was Abraham? How does a nomad gain such favor that he is not only remembered, but revered, 4,000 years after his death? He is claimed by three faiths—Judaism, Islam and Christianity. His seed, as the Scriptures indicate, has become like the sand of the sea and the stars of heaven. Through Isaac he now numbers 13,296,100,[1] and through Ishmael—250 million.[2] And his spiritual seed (Gal. 3:26-29), those who are members of his family by faith, Christians, number 2.1 billion presently on the globe and countless others who are now in heaven.[3] In him, the world finds an intersection. From him comes Jesus, the Messiah.

---

[1] According to the World Jewish Population Survey of 2002, "The size of world Jewry at the beginning of 2002 is assessed at 13,296,100. World Jewry constituted about 2.19 per 1,000 of the world's total population. One in about 457 people in the world is a Jew. According to the revised figures, between 2001 and 2002 the Jewish population grew by an estimated 44,000 people, or about 0.3 percent." The major population centers of the Jewish community are (Table from the World Jewish Population Survey) http://en.wikipedia.org/wiki/Jewish_population

[2] http://en.wikipedia.org/wiki/Arab. The number of adherents to Islam is 1.3 billion. http://www.adherents.com/Religions_By_Adherents.html

[3] http://www.adherents.com/Religions_By_Adherents.html

In Genesis 18, God visits Abraham to further his purposes through the itinerate shepherd. Here the Biblical story makes a critical turn. Pieces fall together. Abraham and Sarah finally are on the same page regarding the vision for a child. A nation is finally to be launched. And Abraham introduces the first example of solemn intercession in all of Scripture. He is standing between God and cities!

Movement One – Entertaining God

In the first movement of the passage, three sojourning men pass by Abraham's camp (Genesis 18:2) near the water-parting route, one of three primary trade routes that stretched north-to-south through Palestine. To the west was the coastal route. To the east, the King's highway.[4] The three travelers appear to be looking for a sip of water and piece of bread. Any hospitality for such travelers was appreciated. Abraham spots them while sitting in his tent door. He goes beyond what would be expected of any host. He prepares a veritable feast. No leftovers will do.

The strangers he entertains are not men. They are angels. And one is no mere angel. One is the Angel of the Lord, the second person of the Trinity, the commander in chief of the army of angels in heaven. Abraham is entertaining angels. No,

4 Charles F. Pfeiffer, Editor. *Baker's Bible Atlas* (Grand Rapids, MI: Baker Books; 1961, 1973), p. 34. The water-parting route was between these two. It ran from Beersheba through Hebron, north-ward through Bethlehem and Jerusalem, onward through the plain of Jezreel where it connected with the coastal route and joined the cities of central Palestine.

14

Abraham is entertaining God! He stands under the oaks where he has spread out the festive table. He stands like a servant. He waits on them as if he were their hired hand. He washes their feet. He entertains their every want. He calls himself their slave.[5] This is prayer!

Prayer is not about words. Nor yet requests. It is not even first and foremost about intercession. That will come. Prayer is about hosting God in a world from which he has been excluded. In prayer, you declare that God is not only welcome, but that He is invited. In prayer, you host him in your heart and your home, the church and your corporation. Prayer says, "God, please don't pass me by! Please let a little water be brought that I might wash your feet! How can I care for your needs, God." Prayer is entertaining God, hosting his presence in a world that is increasingly hostile to him.

Movement Two

The heavenly guests appear to be leaving when the Angel of the Lord enquires about Sarah. He knows she is listening. What is said is for her hearing. Next year, Sarah will have a child. She laughs, but not loud enough to be heard. Ah, but the Angel of the Lord not only hears the laughter of her heart, he reads her private thoughts as well (Genesis 18:12-13).

For years, she has passively resisted the vision of Abraham. For years, she has lived with this dream-

---

5 Charles John Ellicott, editor. *Ellicott's Commentary on the Whole Bible*, Vol. I (Zondervan: Grand Rapids, MI; 1954), 74.

er, tolerating his altar building and the offering of sacrifices, his tales of angelic encounters. She is not hostile to him or his faith. She honors him (1 Peter 3:6). Their marriage is held up as an example for Christian couples, two-thousand years after their death. Peter, in presenting a model of godly marriage in a Greco-Roman world reaches back two- millenniums, back past the Babylonian captivity, the reigns of David and Solomon, the period of the Judges, and the Exodus—back to pre-natal Israel, to Abraham himself. He takes the pre-Hebrew model of Abraham and Sarah, drags it twenty centuries forward, plops it down in the first century and declares, "Here is your model for a godly relationship".

Sarah loves Abraham. She believes, and yet not completely. She has grown to accept her barrenness. She has become comfortable with it. The idea of a child is a closed chapter to her, too painful to open again. She is the realist married to the dreamer. He may still count the stars at night, but she has stopped waiting up for him while knitting an outfit for a newborn. Visions are now for others, for those who are younger. And yet, she is content to be married to this dreamer. After all, his visions are fanciful, but benign.

Abraham has tried substitutions—Eleazer, his servant's children, counted as his own (Genesis 15:2). That suggestion was made to God. And God rejected it. More costly was the suggestion made by Sarah, not to God, but to Abraham. Would that she had asked God about substituting Hagar for herself (Genesis 16:1-2). God would have certainly said, "No!" Instead, she asked Abraham. And he substituted Hagar for his own wife with her unwise support. It was a deadly decision (Genesis 16:3-5). It is not the desire of God to advance covenant purposes in ways that simultaneously violate covenant. Or, to attempt to create a family by acting in ways that destroy one. Abraham was so blindly determined to fulfill the promise that he violated his covenant with Sarah. He was almost as ready to sacrifice Sarah for success of the mission. As Stuart Briscoe acknowledges, "Abraham believed ... but his wife had to believe too."[6] God rejected the action of Abraham with Hagar, and yet left him and his descendents to deal forever with the consequences of his fleshly decision on that fateful afternoon.

Now, 13 years later, God comes by to say to both of them that he has not abandoned his intended purposes. A 24 year old dream is about to come to pass. Sarah will have a child at 90, Abraham at 100. A springtime son will forever change them and the world.

Watch the principle. In entertaining God, the barrenness is broken. In entertaining God, the Angel of the Lord challenges and changes in Sarah what Abraham would never have changed. In entertaining God, the two are brought together in a world-impacting way. Only together, do they find the supernatural life necessary to fulfill their destiny.

---

6 Stuart Briscoe, *The Communicators Commentary - Genesis*; Lloyd J. Ogilvie, General Editor (Word: Waco, TX; 1987), 162.

There are purposes for couples and for families. Purposes for individuals and groups. And there are purposes for cities and nations. In prayer, as we invite the presence of God, He works in us, with us, to move us to the fulfillment of destinies that are latent within us. God confronts couples about their destiny. As churches give themselves to prayer, God reveals his purposes (Acts 13:1-2). As pastors, the elders of a city, gather for prayer, God uncovers destiny for whole regions.

Movement Three

The angels appear to be in the process of leaving again when they mysteriously confer with one another and ask the question, "Shall I hide from Abraham what I am doing?" (Genesis 18:17) First, there was a surprise for Sarah. And now there is one for Abraham. They are headed to Sodom and Gomorrah. Reports have come into heaven regarding the sin of those cities (Genesis 18:20). God will not arbitrarily act. He will investigate. Here is a glimpse into the restraint of God. The patience of Yahweh.

Abraham is about to be told what only heaven knows. He is to be given a look into the future. The destiny of city-states is about to unfold before him. This will not be good news. Sometimes the secrets of God are more of a burden than they are a blessing. Still, God reveals his secrets to the prophets (Amos 3:7). He does nothing in the earth without whispering to his own. On his way to Sodom, to judge the city if necessary, he stops in on an intercessor to whisper secrets no one else in the earth knows.

Here is the point more clearly. Entertaining God invites Him to reveal his secrets to us. Blessed secrets. Cursed secrets. Wonderful news. Dreadful forebodings. Great things. Small items. Dreams. Visions. His mysteries are unwrapped in riddles that slowly unravel over time, their meanings becoming clearer as days and sometimes years go by. He uncovers spirits that lurk behind men and movements. These encounters with God in prayer open up treasures of knowledge we would never know were it not for the initiative of the Spirit.

Movement Four

Sarah will give birth to a son. Abraham will give birth to nation. Sodom and Gomorrah will die. The cities of the plain will perish. And in a few centuries, the sons of Abraham will burst out of Egypt a mighty nation, and settle the land promised to their father. They will worship their way back to the land of milk and honey, with tents raised around the tabernacle of the Lord. In the settled land, they will build a temple and the glory of God will come to rest on that place of worship. They will enthrone a warrior King who will stretch the boundaries of the nation to make it the dominant kingdom in the earth if but for a brief season. But King David will only be a type of the coming King of Kings, and Lord of Lords, Jesus Christ.

Family – The Foundation for God's Purposes

Why Abraham? God declares, "I have known him in order that he might command his family

19

after me. (Genesis 18:19)" The initiative is not with Abraham, it is with God. God's divine disclosure to Abraham has a purpose behind it. He wants to so thoroughly change Abraham, that his sons and daughters will be forever changed. He trusts Abraham to impact his son, and the generations that will follow.

Israel is not primarily a nation – as we think of other nations! It is not merely a land mass with a particular politic. It is a family. That is why it has survived the centuries without a homeland or a geo-political government. Early immigrants to North America often preferred the new identity. Within a generation, they assimilated into the dominant culture. They transitioned from German or French, from Italian or Scandinavian, to English. They fought in two world wars, some against their own homelands. Jewish people have gone centuries living as pilgrims, with a homeland only in their hearts. They have retained customs and identity that anchor their identity and distinctiveness as a people. They are above all else Jews. They are the sons and daughters of Abraham, a pilgrim family in the earth, still searching for a city.

The Church – A Family of Families

Sadly, the Church accommodates to the dominant culture. It fails to retain a distinctive identity. We have made the Church an institution with a program instead of an extended family, a people group, with a purpose. We meet at a certain location for an hour of worship or for various activities. How tragic. The church is neither about a place or a liturgy. It is about collective families, with a mission, called together to bear the presence of God in the earth. The church is lively stones, a living temple, offering constant worship to the Most High God, entertaining him in the earth. The Church gives evidence of the resurrected Christ to an unbelieving world.

As Israel was a family of families, so the Church is a collection of families. The survival of faith in the earth is not dependent upon the verbal skills of our pulpiteers, the organizational skills of our church administrators, nor even the effectiveness of our Christian Educators. It is dependent upon the family.

The Father – His Critical Priestly Role

The faith thrives or dies, based on the integration of values and beliefs, actions and attitudes in our homes. And the central figure that often determines the direction of our homes is the father.

This is why Malachi cries out. "He will turn the hearts of the fathers to the children, and the hearts of the children to the Father" (Malachi 4:6). It is this gender-specific, generational connection between fathers and the children that is so critical to vibrant faith in the earth.

After all they had gone through, God speaks and commands that Abraham take his son, his only son Isaac, who he loved (Genesis 22:2), and go to the land of Moriah where he would act as priest to offer that only Son to the Lord. What did Sarah think he was up to? A camping trip? A father and

21

son outing? Would they return? With what stories to tell? It was a three days journey. Abraham was now living in the land of Gerar and Mt. Moriah was sixty miles northeast. Three days![7] Three days of no contact with the lad. Sarah must have rejoiced when she saw Isaac alive! His name means laughter – what joy there must have been.

Abraham left his servants behind and he and Isaac ascended the mountain together? Did anyone really know what he was up to? What was he thinking? What was Isaac thinking? The boy was loaded down with wood for the fire. Here is the picture of the servant son. A type of Christ, following the Father's will, loaded down with the wood of the cross, headed for his own sacrificial death. We know the types and shadows. Isaac lived, because Christ had, in eternity past, climbed that same mountain, in anticipation of his crucifixion.

The bond between Abraham and Isaac is staggering. The trust of the son in the Father may be reflected no one where else with more clarity than in the relationship of Jesus with the Father. The compliant son, ready to please the Father, on an unquestioning adventure. Abraham, weighted with the potential loss of his Son! Anxious. Confused himself. Would God raise up his son? Would God give him another son?

This experience shaped Isaac. Together, they witnessed the miracle of sacrificial provision.

---

7 M. R. DeHaan. *Protraits of Christ in Genesis* (Zondervan: Grand Rapids, MI; 1966), 135.

Together they worshipped. Together they prayed.
It was a man's thing. It was something so sacred it
could only be shared by a father and son. Servants
had to stand outside this experience.

Hearing God for Your Child
The son is stretched out on the altar of wood he
himself has borne up the mountain. The father has
raised the knife. He is intent on the sacrifice. His
son is already dead in his mind. The blade glistens
in the sunlight. Just as the fatal plunge of the knife
takes place, God speaks.

> *"Abraham, Abraham!" So he said, "Here
> I am." And He said, "Do not lay your
> hand on the lad, or do anything to him;
> for now I know that you fear God, since
> you have not withheld your son, your
> only son, from Me (Genesis 22:11-12).*

Hearing God when he spoke a second time
would have been too late. There are times when
your heart has be so finely turned, that you hear
God with clarity, the first time! Karl Barth
declared,

> In the Church, man is neither a vessel
> of supernatural authority, insight,
> and power, as Roman Catholicism
> teaches, nor is he the free religious
> personality of modern Protestantism
> … Rather, the constitution and pres-

ervation of the Church rests in this,
that man hears God.[8]

Entertaining God readies you to hear God. It sen-
sitizes you to the voice of God. We recognize him
when he speaks. And that may result in the salvation of your son or daughter. It did for Abraham.

> *Abraham lifted his eyes and looked, and
> there behind him was a ram caught in a
> thicket by its horns.*

The lamb is Christ, himself. He dies that Isaac
can live. And in the salvation of Isaac, is our salvation through Jesus, Himself. Here is that wonderful name—The-LORD-Will-Provide, Jehovah Jireh!
And in this provision is a blessing for all the
nations of the earth.

> *So Abraham went and took the ram, and
> offered it up for a burnt offering instead
> of his son. And Abraham called the name
> of the place, The-LORD-Will-Provide; as
> it is said to this day, "In the Mount of
> the LORD it shall be provided." Then
> the Angel of the LORD called to Abraham
> a second time out of heaven, and said:
> "By Myself I have sworn, says the
> LORD, because you have done this thing,
> and have not withheld your son, your
> only son— blessing I will bless you, and*

---

8 McLellan, 38.

*multiplying I will multiply your descen-
dants as the stars of the heaven and as
the sand which is on the seashore; and
your descendants shall possess the gate
of their enemies. In your seed all the
nations of the earth shall be blessed,
because you have obeyed My voice"
(Genesis 22:13-18).*

Marking Our Families for Generations

We don't know what Isaac told his sons about
their grandfather and grandmother. We only know
Abraham emerges as such a powerful figure that
400 years of slavery cannot stamp out his memory.
He becomes larger than life. His relationship with
God inspires his children to this day. His favor
with God and the family distinctive born of that
favor, sparked a slave revolt like none other in history. And the sons and daughters of Abraham, left
Egypt and came home to the Fatherland.

Sarah had a son. Abraham gave birth to a
nation.

Is it possible, that by entertaining God, you and
I might procure the favor of God upon generations? Is it possible, that I might leave behind some
blessing for my children and grandchildren? Is it
possible that God looks at me, and remembers the
prayers prayed for me by my godly grandfather?
Could I bless my children, ten generations hence,
should Jesus tarry, by entertaining God in a world
that consistently expels them? Could I invite the
favor of God upon my children's children.

25

Watch what happens to Abraham's son Isaac.

*Isaac sowed ... and reaped in the same
year a hundredfold; the LORD blessed
him. The man ... became very prosperous; he had possessions of flocks and possessions of herds and a great number of
servants.*

*The Philistines stopped up all the wells
which his father had dug ... And Isaac
dug again the wells of water ... Then he
went up to Beersheba. And the LORD
appeared to him the same night and said,
"I am the God of your father Abraham;
do not fear, for I am with you. I will bless
you and multiply your descendants **for
My servant Abraham's sake.**" Genesis
23:12-15, 23-24.*

Movement Five

The final movement of Genesis 18 is the first
introduction of solemn intercession in all of
Scripture. Having learned that the angels are on a
mission of exploration which could result in tragedy for Sodom, Abraham does something daring.
He steps between the Angel of the Lord and the
plight of the cities of the plain. His actions are
exemplary. But it is his attitude that is most reveal-
ing.

For many the news that Sodom was about get its
due might have met with approval. Not so with

Abraham. And this is a twist that cannot be over-looked. Here Abraham is stirred to grace and mercy. He is not ready to strike the first match. He finds no joy in the news of impending judgment even if the target of that punishment is a sinful set of cities like Sodom and Gomorrah.

> *"Shall not the judge of the earth do right?" (Genesis 18:25)*

Pleading for the Honor of God

His plea is not merely for his nephew, even though Lot may be on his mind. We *should* be moti-vated to plead for the salvation of our loved ones when they are in harms way. But the construct of his prayer is not out of his narrow interest in his nephew or even the city. He is concerned about the honor of God!

This is something rare in modern praying. Most of us are motivated by our own narrow slice of pain. Rarely do we hear prayers which rally the active intervention or restrain of God in view of His character and honor. The notion is almost for-eign to us. And yet, this is the basis of Abraham's plea. And this was the basis of the plea of Moses when he stepped between God and Israel to restrain the judgment of God (Genesis 18:23).

Maybe such a notion is foreign to us, because we see such texts as an indictment of God. Moses and Abraham seem to be more merciful than God. They seem to be restraining an angry God. "Claim down, God. No fire, not here, not now. Back off!"

27

Such scenes seem to make Moses and Abraham the cool and reasonable heads that balance a hot-headed, fire-breathing God.

So with such embarrassing dynamics potentially happening, we ignore these passages. What God is wanting to do is exactly the opposite. He is wanting to wake up the intercessor in Abraham and later in Moses. He wants them to stand between him and judgment, as intercessors are supposed to do.

Waking Up Grace

Sin wakes up the wrath of God, but intercession wakes up his grace. When Christ steps between death and life, it is not to appease an angry God. He intercedes. He calls forth the grace of the Father, tapping into potential forgiveness for every honest and repentant soul. Intercession does this. It weeps over sin. It recognizes the power of evil. It sees death's hold. And simultaneously, it lays hold of life. Watchman Nee observes,

> Prayer is not just asking God for something. For the church to pray means that it stands on God's side to declare that man wants what God wants.[9]

When sin abounds, God reveals his forgotten holiness to his holy leaders. He manifests his righ-

9 Watchman Nee. *The Prayer Ministry of the Church* (Living Stream Ministry: Anaheim, CA; 1993), 13.

teous indignation to his righteous followers. Where does Jesus flash with anger? Not in the town square of a Roman capital! But in the temple. "My house shall be a house of prayer for the nations! You have made it a den of thieves. (Luke 19:46)" God reveals his anger to those who should resonate with it. "Yes, God! We are as grieved as you are over the sin around us! Yes, God!" This should lead us to cry out against the sin that abounds, because we know that sin will ultimately meet judgment. What it needs now, is grace. Grace that leads to repentance.

Intercession – the Prophetic and the Priestly

There are two dimensions to intercession. One is prophetic. The other is priestly. Neither is ever complete without the other. The prophetic sees. It uncovers. It reveals. It forecast consequences. It challenges. It moves to repentance. It champions holiness, righteousness and justice. The priestly also sees. It isn't blind. But rather than expose the sin and cry against it, the priest seeks to cover it with grace. To conceal. To create the bridge for reconciliation with God on the back of genuine repentance. to preserve what sin might have completely destroyed.

The prophetic is confrontational. The priestly is conciliatory. The prophetic champions truth. The priestly champions love and forgiveness. The prophetic seeks to prevent that which affronts the holiness of God. The priestly seeks to promote that which affirms the grace and the love of God. The prophetic articulates his consuming holiness. The priestly, his encompassing compassion.

When intercessors recognize both the sin of the culture, and simultaneously the righteousness of God, and then prayerfully cry out for a revival of righteousness based on repentance, they sanctify working space for God. This is the ground on which the grace of God abundantly works. God wakes up intercessors to a crisis of unrighteousness. Their cry for righteousness voices what God longs to hear from the earth. And the result is grace!

Abraham appeals to the honor of God! He is concerned about the reputation of God in the earth. So little of our intercession bears this burden. "God, you must show up! Your reputation is at stake!" Such a prayer must be offered in a humble way. This is not an attempt to blackmail God. He never acts because he is reading popularity polls.

The concern over his honor is tied to other themes—his name, his glory. Abraham is concerned that the earth will gain the wrong picture of God. He wants God to act in ways, not that please him, but in ways that promote the broader purposes to which God is committed. He is an advocate in behalf of God. And at the same time, a kind of interpreter from the earth – "Here is how it looks down here!" The process is not to inform God. It is a discovery experience for Abraham, the intercession!

The Intercessor: A Spiritual Ambassador

In an international crisis, an ambassador is valuable not only as a go-between, which is the essence of the intercessor. We are here on the earth as ambassadors of another kingdom (Proverbs 13:17; Jeremiah 49:14; 2 Corinthians 5:20; Ephesians 6:20). And there is a war between heaven and earth (Acts 4:26). So our role as spokesmen in the earth is critical. In that sense, we represent God to the nation and nations. We may speak to kings (Matthew 10:18; Mark 13:9; Luke 10:24; 21:12; 1 Timothy 2:2).

The ambassador, like the intercessor, stands between. He communicates between the parties. He carries messages from the earth to the King of Heaven, and from God to the nations. In this position – we represent both parties. We are earthlings, but our hearts and our citizenship is in heaven. We resonate the values of God's kingdom in our prayer. But we cry out in behalf of the pain and spiritual-moral disconnect around us in the earth. Like Paul, we have a desire to depart, to go home to heaven. But then, we are caught up in the need of the earth around us (Philippians 1:23).

As ambassadors, we not only carry the raw content, the facts, of the problems that besiege our world, we characterize it. We represent its people, feel its mood, weep over its pain, plead for its promise. This light is more than the delivery of a message. The ambassador enters into dialogue on how to respond in a way that defuses the crisis and promotes reconciliation and peace. The intercessor-ambassador is laying before his own King the alternatives to interpret the situation and explore alternatives. He offers the perspective of the earth,

31

the way the actions of the King will be seen by the earth. He serves as lens, an alternative perspective of the situation.

So Abraham pleads,

- *"Would you destroy the righteous with the wicked?"* (Genesis 18:23) Abraham argues that the value of God's care for the righteous must supersede his judgment. God's love must triumph! God agrees! Abraham then presses the issue. How much mercy can be garnered in the face of an utterly wicked place, with a handful of righteous souls.

- *"Suppose there were fifty righteous within the city; would You also **destroy** the place and not spare it for the fifty righteous that were in it?"* (Genesis 18:24) He barters until the number is down to ten? Who knows how far he might have gone? Who knows how far God's grace might have reached? To one? For the sake of one, Jesus Christ, God has decided to spare our world and restrain judgment (Romans 5:18-19). The powerful precedent is established here for all intercessors. The favor of God extends to the wicked, because of the presence of the righteous among them.

- *"Far be it from You to do such a thing as
  this, to slay the righteous with the wicked,
  so that the righteous should be as the
  wicked; far be it from You! Shall not the
  Judge of all the earth do right?"*(Genesis
  18:25). Now Abraham appeals for
  grace, not merely in terms of the presence of the righteous in the target area
  of judgment, but in terms of the character of God Himself. This is powerful
  reasoning. Abraham is not saying,
  "Hold your fire! My nephew is there.
  The righteous might be injured!"
  More is at stake than the protection of
  a small band of the just. God's honor
  is at stake. "You cannot do this! This is
  not consistent with your character.
  You must do righteously, and this
  potential action is not righteous!"

Prayer – God's Classroom

God does not need to be informed. He knows
the hearts of all men. Prayer is the context in which
we are mentored. We come to see things as He sees
them. We interpret the actions of nations, the
words of kings. As we come to understand Him in
a deeper way, we represent Him more effectively
here on the earth. Learning to pray in a way that
promotes the honor of God gives us greater influence.

Abraham begins this chapter by entertaining
God. And he ends with influence over nations.

The Five Movements Reviewed

Five movements. Prayer is entertaining God. Hosting his presence. And that opens the closed womb of promise. It breaks the barrenness. God whispers secrets we would have no other way of knowing, were it not for the fact that we had spent time with Him. Blessings come upon our family— for generations. We procure the favor of God. And after we die, God takes care of our children and grandchildren! Finally, posturing as a servant, longing to do nothing but please God, we end up with influence over city-nations!

No wonder Paul admonished us, "Consider Abraham!" (Galatians 3:6).

MOVEMENT ONE

Prayer as Entertaining God

Genesis 18:1-8

Then the Lord appeared to him by the terebinth trees of Mamre, as he was sitting in the tent door in the heat of the day. So he lifted his eyes and looked, and behold, three men were standing by him; and when he saw them, he ran from the tent door to meet them, and bowed himself to the ground, and said, "My Lord, if I have now found favor in Your sight, do not pass on by Your servant. Please let a little water be brought, and wash your feet, and rest yourselves under the tree. And I will bring a morsel of bread, that you may refresh your hearts. After that you may pass by, inasmuch as you have come to your servant."

They said, "Do as you have said."

So Abraham hurried into the tent to Sarah and said, "Quickly, make ready three measures of fine meal; knead it and make cakes." And Abraham ran to the herd, took a tender and good calf, gave it to a young man, and he hastened to prepare it. So he took butter and milk and the calf which he had prepared, and set it before them; and he stood by them under the tree as they ate.

The Transformation of the Olmos Prison

Juan Zuccarelli and Jos Tessi convinced the authorities at the Olmos Prison to permit evangelistic services. The fourth floor of the prison was such a powerful center of occult worship that it was affecting the entire nation of Argentina. Inmates sacrificed animals and conducted satanic rituals. The prison had become a training center for the dark arts. Inmates who had been baptized into the occult arts were often transferred to other prisons. The sickness spread throughout the criminal element in the nation. When these new cultic priests were released, the whole culture was corrupted.

Cell-by-cell evangelism first reached a small core of men. Forty Christians could be found among the 2,000 inmates. At their first evangelistic meeting, 300 inmates attended and 100 of them committed their lives to Christ. A movement had begun. Within the next two years, the seeds of revival spread. Whole cell blocks came under the influence of the gospel. Soon, each of the five floors consisting of 12 cell blocks had Christian influence. The prison staff then moved all the Christians to one floor—the fourth floor, which had been controlled by the occult group in the prison. Now, half the cell blocks on that floor were filled with Christians, the other half with occult advocates.

The Christians organized themselves into a church they named "Christ the Only Hope!" Five years later, they had 400 members. In another three years, 900 inmates were believers. In the next two years, their number grew to 1,200. The prison population had a 10 percent per year turnover. As these Christians were transferred to other penal institutions throughout the nation, they became as influential in the network of prisons as the occult group had been.

What was the secret to the transformation of the prison? How could they so effectively reach hardened criminals and break through the bondage of the occult? Prayer! The ministry itself had been birthed out of the prayer walks of Juan Zuccarelli, an Assembly of God pastor turned prison guard. And Christ the Only Hope Church required all active members to be part of the church's prayer focus. Corporate prayer meetings were held every night of the week with all members expected to participate. In addition, they maintained a prayer watch. Every member participated by taking part in a three-hour prayer watch sometime in the midnight-to-6 a.m. time frame. They prayed for the other inmates. They worshiped. They went from bed to bed quietly praying for all the prisoners to whom they had access. Not less than 120 men were involved in the prayer watch every night! Some cellblocks organized 24/7 prayer.[1]

They were entertaining God. And He came to the prison, changed its atmosphere, saved hardened criminals and priests of the occult, and impacted the nation. Entertaining God influences nations.

[1] Dick Eastman, Beyond Imagination (Grand Rapids: Chosen Books—a division of Baker, 1997) 113-5.

1

ENTERTAINING ANGELS
UNAWARE

Have you ever been to Nowhere? It is a small town on the border of New Mexico and the Texas panhandle. Nowhere! To get to Nowhere you have to be going there! Not so with Hebron, at least in Bible times. It is one of the ancient cities in the world located on a primary trade route, about 20 miles south-southwest of Jerusalem. Three thousand feet above sea level in the Judean hill country, it is the highest point in the region, rising 4,300 feet above the Dead Sea a few miles away. Around it was a fertile countryside filled with vineyards and orchards. Mamre, Abraham's campsite, was two miles north of Hebron.[1]

It happened just after the noon meal, in the heat

---

[1] Allen Myers, ed., *The Eerdmans Bible Dictionary*: "Hebron" (Grand Rapids: Eerdmans, 1987) 476.

of the day around siesta time; a lazy afternoon. Sarah had retired to the compartment in the back of the Bedouin-style tent. But Abraham chose to sit in the doorway of his tent, the flap raised, providing a measure of shade from the sun. Nearby was a grove of terebinth trees, a species of oak. One of them is still alive today, more than 5,000 years old. It is a landmark in Hebron, near Abraham's burial place. The oak might have provided a more hospitable place for a nap, but with Sarah sleeping in the back of the tent, he sat in the doorway, the threshold, the place of covenant.

Unexpectedly, three visitors appeared on the horizon.

Entertaining Strangers

In the ancient world, travelers were greatly reliant on the kindness offered them by the residents of the arid land through which they traveled. And yet hosting strangers had its risks, as Lot would discover (Genesis 19). Provision was more than a handout. It was also a pledge to protect. A sojourner was dependent upon the hospitable people he would meet along the way. Without the help of kind folks, he would never reach his destination. They advised him. They had inside local information on the road conditions, hostile points on the journey, distances to the next freshwater well. Sometimes they even entered into a covenant with travelers. So a traveler might skirt the edge of a camp to test the possibility of such invaluable hospitality.

These visitors stopped a good distance from Abraham's camp and stood silently, as if waiting for some cue that would provide permission for them to advance into Abraham's camp or proceed on their journey around the periphery looking for hospitality elsewhere.

Abraham rose, as if to signal that he saw the migrating party. Sometimes a potential host would move toward the traveling party in an investigative mode. He might bow to show respect or exchange greetings. If hospitality was offered, both the level and extent of it would be at the discretion of the host. Whatever the host gave would be of his own volition, and the refusal of his gifts would be a great insult. His gestures would grant permission for the visitors to enter the territory of his camp with the unstated promise of safety.

Abraham threw caution aside. He raced through all of these steps. He ran to meet the three travelers. He bowed, demonstrating deference. He insisted that they not pass him by. He reversed the typical scenario. Normally, the travelers were indebted to the host for the hospitality offered. They were at the mercy of the host. Their survival depended upon the kindness offered, water and bread (perhaps milk and meat). But Abraham acted toward the nomads as if he would be the unfortunate one were they to pass by.

He bowed. He begged for the privilege of serving

41

them. Who were these nomads? They were not mere men; they were angels. And one of them was no mere angel. He was the Angel of Yahweh. The writer of Hebrews reminds us, "Some have entertained angels unawares!" (13:2, KJV). There are 30 references in Scripture regarding the treatment of strangers. Abraham apparently knew—if not on sight, shortly into his encounter with these three—that they were not mere men. He promised "a little water...a morsel of bread" (Genesis 18:4, 5). It is a gross understatement of his intentions. When he returned to his tent, he ordered a feast—three measures of fine meal baked in cakes, a tender and good calf, butter and milk (vv. 6-8). Some scholars suggest the language is purposely "self-deprecating," an indication of his true humility.[2]

Entertaining Angels Unaware

The Angel of Yahweh is the angel who appeared to Gideon (Judges 6:11). He is the Man who wrestled with Jacob (Genesis 32:24-30). He was the fourth man in the fiery furnace (Daniel 3:25). This Angel was one of the riders who appeared to Zechariah outside Jerusalem in the season of the city's restoration (Zechariah 1:11). And this is the Angel who appeared to Joshua outside the walls of the fortress city of Jericho before the battle that would give the Promised Land

---

[2] Adele Berlin, Marc Zvi Brettler and Michael Fishbane, eds., *The Jewish Study Bible* (New York: Oxford UP; The Jewish Publication Society, 2004) 39.

into the hands of Israel, the first conquest after the 40 years of wilderness wandering (Joshua 5:13, 14).

Joshua would be commanded to remove his shoes before this Angel and worship. No mere angel is worthy of our worship (Colossians 2:18). The Scripture forbids it. But this is not a mere angel. This is the Angel of the Lord. He is the Commander-in-Chief of the army of angels in heaven. He is the second person of the Trinity; the Word, who became flesh (John 1:1-3, 14). This is the One we know as Jesus in His preincarnate, angelic form.[3]

Abraham exclaimed, "If I have *now* found favor in Your sight, do not pass on by Your servant" (Genesis 18:3). The appearance of the angel of the Lord was only three days after the circumcision of Abraham. He had complied with the commandment of the Lord regarding circumcision. He had done his part. Now, he was asking, "Have I *now* found favor?" This obedient man was so anxious to please God. The covenant was one of faith, but the fruit of faith is always obedience. Faith acts. And "faith without works is dead" (see James 2:17). It is not faith *plus* works, but faith *that* works. What is the connection between faith and obedience? It is first, discerning the Lord's presence. And second, hearing in that encounter the voice of

---

[3] See J. Barton Payne's work, *The Theology of the Older Testament* (Grand Rapids: Zondervan, 1962) 167. A helpful section on the angel of the Lord.

the Lord with a heart bent toward obedience. When the Bible says that we are "to hear," it always means to "hear and obey!"

Jewish tradition says the visit to the patriarch was a healing mission.[4] And once healed, the angel of the Lord returned to nudge Sarah and Abraham toward the fulfillment of their destiny. Abraham could have had no clue on that sleepy afternoon how profound, how world-changing this encounter with God would be. He was not the seeker; God was seeking him. But as always, our Lord wants an invitation to enter our camp. History turned that day when Abraham entertained God.

You and I have no real perception about the power of hosting God's presence. Such moments change us, they change history—and we may not even realize how profound our encounters with the presence of God really are until we stand in heaven.

Ira Sankey was the soloist for D.L. Moody. Traveling on a steamboat, he was invited to sing a song for the passengers. He sang the old hymn "Savior, Like a Shepherd Lead Us." When he had finished, a passenger called him over and inquired if he had served military time in the war between the states. "Yes," he

---

[4] Charles John Ellicott, ed., *Ellicott's Commentary on the Whole Bible*, Vol. I (Grand Rapids: Zondervan, 1954) 73. Some have said the number *three* points to the Trinity in the Godhead, and as a result this passage is read in liturgical churches on Trinity Sunday. Ellicott says the suggestion is an inference only and to insist on such would be "heretical impiety."

replied. "On which side?" the passenger queried. "The North," he responded. More questions followed—"What year? Where? Did you ever pull picket duty there?" "Yes," Ira replied to all the questions. The passenger grew quiet. He explained, "I was a Confederate. I remember the moonlit night when I saw you. I had you in my sights to shoot you. As I squeezed the trigger, you raised your eyes toward heaven and you began to sing the same song you have just sung here tonight. I thought, *Let him sing his song—then I'll shoot him.* But when you finished singing the song, I was unable to do my soldierly task. Sir, I have never met the Gentle Shepherd, and I need a cure for my soul." Sankey threw his arms around him and told him about Jesus.[5]

Entertaining God is a powerful thing. It may save your life. It may bring you under His protective care. It may transform the hearts of others intent on hurting you, perhaps destroying you.

This page is so good

---

[5] Bill Thrasher, *A Journey to Victorious Praying* (Chicago: Moody, 2003) 207-8.

2

RECOGNIZING GOD'S
PRESENCE

In Matthew 14, Jesus fed the 5,000. It was quite a
miracle. And as He often did, He left the scene of
public power to retreat to private prayer. His miracles
were hemmed in by prayer. His days began and ended
in prayer.

He sent His disciples ahead to cross the Sea of
Galilee (v. 22). He would join them later. He prayed
and prayed through the night. In the fourth watch
of the night, between 3 and 6 a.m., He caught a vision
of His disciples. They were toiling, rowing, caught
in a vicious storm. What should have been a short
and routine trip for these veteran fishermen who
knew the sea and its shoreline from memory was,
instead, a night like they had never experienced.

Storms on the Sea of Galilee are sudden and quite
violent. A few years ago, Barbara and I were in a small

boat on that sea. Spontaneously, she sang, "He is here, Alleluia!" and then, "Peace, peace, wonderful peace!" Others softly joined in that song. Then the fog rolled in. The thunder rumbled above us, and we headed for shelter. Seated in a lakeside restaurant, eating Saint Peter's fish, the storm broke with pounding rain, mixed with hailstones, rumbling thunder and flashing lightning. In what seemed like a matter of minutes, the weather on the Sea of Galilee had changed dramatically.

Life's Sudden Spiritual Storms

The storm that trapped the disciples on the sea for almost 12 hours seems to have a spiritual edge about it. It appears to be more than a mere natural phenomenon. That storm did not come and go—it endured. The disciples became disoriented. In prayer, Jesus saw them. This was not natural seeing. Visibility, due to the weather and the darkness of the night, would have been zero. He saw in the Spirit, through the lens of prayer.

At times, we may feel that God has abandoned us. Our storms can seem so intense. A miracle day turns into a midnight nightmare. Life, it appears, will be strangled by death. How strange! God's power was so clearly demonstrated in the feeding of the 5,000. He was care and compassion incarnate, wrapped up in power and provision. Here was God, the "manna-maker," on the scene. Here was Christ, who insisted that no one leave hungry. So caring. So sensitive.

So confident. So commanding. Everyone was cared for. All were full and satisfied. The natural limitations were laid aside by the supernatural work of God in Christ. Wow! And there were leftovers, besides (v. 20). There was more than enough.

A few hours later, the natural roared back to a test of faith in the miraculous. Of what value is the provision of the day if we perish in the night? No miracle is completely yours until you can hold on to its meaning in the midst of despair. Light is *meant* to be taken into darkness. Hope is *intended* to gobble up despair. Spirit-life is never fully tested until it faces death and refuses to blink.

Where is Jesus when such tests come to us? He is on the mountain in heaven—God's mountain—Mount Zion. And He sees us toiling and rowing. He is praying for us. When no one else is praying for you, He ever lives to make intercession for you (Romans 8:34; Hebrews 7:25).

But He does more. He came to the disciples, walking on the water. The sure sign of an impending shipwreck to an ancient mariner was the sighting of a ghost, a phantom, on the water in the midst of a storm. The disciples lifted their eyes. With visibility near zero, they imagined that they were seeing a mirage. Something was out there. Some*one* was out there. Impossible. On the water? In a storm? The vision became clearer. It was unmistakably a human shape. The robe of the mysterious, shadowy figure blew in the fierce wind. Whoever was out there was standing. But what on? There was no boat, no vessel of any kind.

Striding forward across the sea and against the wind as if undaunted by it, the figure moved parallel to their vessel. Heart rhythms increased. Blood pressures rose. Nervous glances were exchanged, but no one said a word. It was Jesus on the water. Every disciple recognized Him. All must have doubted their own eyes. None dared give voice to confirm the supposed apparition. Then Peter broke the tense silence. He cried out, choosing to believe that what he saw was no mirage. Every one of his comrades was simultaneously relieved and rattled. They were relieved that they were not seeing things; they were rattled in the wonder of how Jesus could be on the water in the midst of the storm without a boat.

Peter was beyond all that. He actively engaged Christ. "If it is You, command me to come to You on the water" (Matthew 14:28). Jesus bid him come. Almost immediately, before he could be restrained by fellow disciples, Peter was out of the boat and walked on the water.

J. Oswald Chambers says prayer "invests puny men with a sort of omnipotence."[1] Peter was thrusting himself into the arms of Jesus. That is what prayer does. Peter discovered something we have yet to acknowledge. He was safer on the water with Jesus in the midst of such a storm than he was in a boat

---

[1] Bill Thrasher, *A Journey to Victorious Praying* (Chicago: Moody, 2003) 134.

without Jesus. Yes, he would momentarily lose his focus. He would see the storm and not the Savior. The wind and waves would become more real to him than Christ. Yes, he sank and became overwhelmed by the fierce howling gale, the lightning dancing on the unstable waves. Yes, he doubted and began to descend into dark waters, but the waves could not consume him. The storm would not claim him. There would be no watery grave for Peter. In those few moments when Jesus and the other world were more real than things one can touch and feel, Peter walked on the water. And when he sank, Jesus graciously lifted him up, and together, they entered the boat. Only then did the storm cease.

O. Hallesby, an influential Christian teacher in Norway, recognized prayer as posture. He saw it as the attitude of the heart out of the position of helplessness—not a helplessness that leads to anxiety, but a desperation that drives us to dependence upon God.[2] Even as Peter sank, he was safe! Even in a momentary crisis of faith, grace saved him. E.M Bounds declares, "Prayer honors God; it dishonors self. It is man's plea of weakness, ignorance, want; a plea which heaven cannot disregard. God delights to have us pray."[3]

The Necessity of Prayer

There is one small note we have overlooked. Jesus,

[2] Thrasher, 19.

[3] E.M. Bounds, *The Complete Works of E.M. Bounds on Prayer* (Grand Rapids: Baker, 1990) 319. Quoted by Paul Cedar, *A Life of Prayer* (Nashville: Word, 1998) 13.

the Scripture says, "would have passed them by" (Mark 6:48). What a mystery. He comes near us. But to come to us, He awaits our invitation. How many times are we left in our storms because we do not invoke His name or cry out, "Lord! Is that You? Let me come to You! Lord, don't pass me by!"

There are times when God comes walking through our troubled campsite. He stands in the middle of our storm while we are being tossed to and fro, rapidly taking on water. In such moments, He wants to be recognized and invited into the crisis. He is looking for those who will entertain Him and not allow the storm to so rattle them, that they lose the awareness of God's presence in the middle of the problem. Into every predicament, God interjects Himself as the solution. He waits to be discovered. When He is ignored, He moves on. He passes by.

In Genesis 18, the same idea is implied. The angels would have passed by Abraham's camp had he not appealed to them to accept his hospitality (v. 3). Our God longs to be invited into an encounter with us. He can kick down the doors of our lives—and sometimes He does. He can knock a stubborn and wrongly determined rabbi who was persecuting the church off his donkey and blind him for a few days of personal reassessment, but He prefers to encounter us on the ground of love, not force.

Real-Life Encounters With Jesus

Example One: The mood in the emergency waiting

area is somber. Lives are dangling by a thread. Nerves are frayed. Tears are common. Tension is high. The right words come stubbornly in such settings. Then Jesus walks through the room. He is simultaneously out of place, and exactly in position. With Him is comfort from another world. But someone has to entertain Him, invoke His name. Someone has to prevent Him from merely passing through the room.

The moment is often as difficult for us as it was for Peter to take the first step out of the boat. It is that first step that moves you from this realm to the other. It is those first words that seem like a foreign language that gives life in place of death; hope in such despair; peace with confusion and uncertainty so real that their voices can be heard echoing up and down the halls. The first step is so difficult, but the pathway from tragedy to triumph is always a faith walk. You slip into the chair next to the grieving mother. You take her hand and pray a simple prayer. Others huddle around you. Jesus is there.

Example Two: You are in the middle of a mad quarrel where voices are raised and tempers are flaring. You are already saying things you don't mean. If this continues, you will damage an already stressed relationship. You have been under such pressure because of so many reverses compounding all at once. Now, in the stress created by fear, you are acting out of impulse. Your verbal assaults are veiled pleas for help, but neither party has the words of

use at church

53

hope to calm the accelerating anxieties. Suddenly, you sense Jesus. Yes, you sense Him in the middle of a family fight, just as clearly as you sensed Him in church a few weeks ago, Easter morning, when the choir sang, "He is risen." You thought you heard Him whisper to you, "I have! I have risen—and I have come to show you how real I am and how much I love you!"

You had never received a message like that before. It was like someone invisible brushed you, and then whispered to you. You remember the moment. You looked around, but no one was there. It raised the goose bumps all right. Now you sense that same presence again. It is Jesus. He is in the room. He is alive, and He loves you. He loves us! You remember what the pastor said: "Prayer is simple. You just cry out to God."

You shock your spouse with an embrace as you cry out aloud, "Jesus. We need Your help! Lord Jesus, reveal Yourself to us." You see the intrigued and simultaneously skeptical look on the face of your partner. Are you having a nervous breakdown? Are you kidding with them? Are you trying to sidetrack the argument? Are you serious? You say nothing. You take your spouse into your arms and pray spontaneously. It is a simple prayer with no flowery words. It's a desperate prayer, with passion: "Lord Jesus, have mercy on us! Save us! We have no one else to turn to. We are in a storm with waves over our heads."

Suddenly, something is different. Nothing has changed, but everything has changed. The room looks the same. There is no flash of lightning, no thunder, no voice, and yet it is so clear that something is different. The problem remains before you, but it is no longer the dominant feature. You sense His presence. He has not spoken, but deep inside you know that He has heard you and help is on the way. You can't explain it, but you know it. You invoked His name; He did not pass you by.

Example Three: The metal and glass are everywhere. The smoke is still rising from the vehicles. The accident scene is littered with the debris of vehicles that moments ago had collided. Drivers and passengers are dazed. Human inventories are quickly taken. "Are you all right?" a mother asks her children. *Am I all right?* she asks herself. *Are the folks in the other car OK?* You arrive on the scene seconds after the accident happens. The dust has not yet settled. People are shaken. Other cars navigate around and through the field of debris. Someone quickly lays out flares and begins to direct traffic. In the distance, you faintly hear the sirens. Emergency personnel are on the way. Suddenly, you sense Jesus. He is here. He is walking through the debris, waiting for someone, yet not just anyone, to invite Him to "not pass by!" You walk over to one of the vehicles. The driver is still inside—dazed and shaken. The injuries, miraculously, appear to be minor. You say, "Emergency vehicles have been called. Is there anything I can do for you? Is there someone I can call on your behalf?" You sense their need of time to regain their personal equilibrium. "Look, I am a Christian!" They make eye contact with you—real eye contact. You continue, "I am a Christian, and right now I am praying for you! Could I pray aloud for you?" You don't even wait for permission; you know it's OK. You begin to invoke the name of Jesus, recognizing His presence. You appeal to the Prince of Peace, to give peace. While you pray, you hold the hand of the person and quote a psalm. You assure him or her, in the language of faith and hope, that all is well. You have refused to let the Lord pass by! And He climbs into the mangled vehicle and declares His lordship. He whispers to the storm. He quiets the hearts.

3

HOSTING GOD IN THE EARTH

D r. Bob May impacted my life. He was one of my Bible college professors. But it was his passion for Jesus that infected my life in ways I would not completely understand until years had passed. I have forgotten other teachers, but I will never forget Dr. May. His habit was to amble into the classroom with his ukulele under his arm. Most of the time, he seemed more interested in loving Jesus than motivating us to love theology.

- I was about information; he was about forma-tion.
- I was looking for preaching material; he was trying to make preacher material out of me.
- I wanted principles; he offered God's presence.

What an impact he had on my life.

John Fischer says:

> The problem is not how well Satan has coun-
> terfeited Christianity, but how far Christianity
> has digressed from its central focus in search
> for the pragmatic. Making life work, being suc-
> cessful, answering questions, feeling good, and
> solving problems have become more impor-
> tant to the modern Christian than knowing
> and worshiping the true God.[1]

Paul Rees says:

> Let philosophers wrestle with the idea of God,
> and theologians with the attributes of God,
> and scientists with the works of God; but as
> for me, being interested in the inner and sus-
> taining vitality of religion, nothing can satisfy
> me short of the realized presence of God.[2]

Dr. May was an evangelist in the role of a teacher—
and oh how his fervor for Jesus came through. He
opened a coffee shop in the heart of Fresno, California,
in the days of the youth revolution. It was not a retail
establishment, it was a youth outreach. Hundreds,
maybe thousands, of kids were saved. The crowds
sometimes overflowed with teens spilling out not
only onto the sidewalks, but also into the busy down-
town Fresno streets.

Then there were the stories about his nighttime
adventures into the city that so intrigued us. He
would take his ukulele into a collection of the darkest

---

[1] Quoted by Vernon McLellan, *Thoughts That Shaped the Church* (Wheaton: Tyndale, 2000) 25.

[2] Quoted by McLellan, 117.

and seamiest bars in the city. This is not the kind of thing you would expect from your typical Bible college professor.

Entering a bar, he would lay his instrument case on the counter and order a 7-Up. An inebriated individual would cajole the bartender into letting Dr. May sing a song. The whole atmosphere of the bar would change as he sang one of his favorites: "I'm walking and talking with my mind, stayed on Jesus!" Out of the darkened corners of the bar would come requests for another religious song. "Can you sing 'Amazing Grace'?" The whole bar might end up singing. Backslidden preachers would crawl out of those booths, their lives now in shambles.

Bob May was entertaining God. He was not a great musician. It was his heart that did the singing. He was a traveling temple, radiating God's glory. His humility, offered in bold faithfulness, invited God's presence to break into places where He was typically ignored and often dishonored.

Prayer is more than a means of acquisition. The greatest feat of prayer is to lay hold of the light and life of God, opening a door for His presence to break into places of darkness. Dr. May was about God's presence.

A.W. Tozer says:

> We have lost the art of worship. We are not producing saints. Our models are successful businessmen, celebrated athletes, and theatrical personalities. We carry on our religious activities

after the methods of the modern advertisers. Our homes have been turned into theaters, our literature is shallow, our hymns border on sacrilege, and scarcely anyone seems to care. Christianity is little more than objective truth, sweetened with song and made palatable through religious entertainment. Christ calls men to carry a cross, but we call them to have fun in His name.[3]

Amy Carmichael challenges us with these words:

I believe that if we are to be and do for others what God means us to be and do, we must not let adoration and worship slip into second place, for it is the central thing asked by God of human souls, and its neglect is responsible for much lack of spiritual depth and power .... And so we are shallow; a wind, quite a little wind, can ruffle our surface; a little hot sun, and all the moisture in us evaporates. It should not be so.[4]

Making Dinner for God

It was midday and the sun was beating down on the ancient oak of Mamre, already at that time 1,000 years old. What stories that oak could tell! Abraham's camp set in a shallow valley, 3,000 feet above sea level and 4,300 feet (1,310 meters) above the nearby Dead Sea.

---

[3] Quoted by McLellan, 264.

[4] Quoted by Bob Walz, Sue Swett, Tracy McKenzie; ed. Bob Walz, *Kingdom Culture 101* (*http://navscanada.gospelcom.net/UofM/resources/Kingdomc.pdf*).

read on Sun, Drun.

As strangers approached the camp of Abraham, he rose from his tent door. Then he ran to meet them. The phrase "Abraham drew near" (Genesis 18:23, KJV) is used specifically for prayer![5] Yet, as Thomas Merton observes, "We could not seek God unless He were seeking us."[6] He comes by us, wanting to come near us—if we will respond to Him.

At first, Abraham offered the travelers a morsel of bread. But immediately after encountering these strangers, he called for a feast. He knew! These were not mere men. This was the third time he had met with the Angel of the Lord. The first encounter had been to give him the promise, 24 years before (see 12:1-7). The second encounter had broken 13 silent years after the fleshly liaison with Hagar (ch. 16). The silence must have seemed like an eternity.

Weeks before the three visitors appeared, at the age of 99, the Angel of the Lord had come to him for the second time and reaffirmed Yahweh's 24-year-old commitment (ch. 17). He had fallen on his face in reverence (v. 3). God had made things so clear. He had a part. Abram had a part—circumcision. And Sarai had a part—she would have to bear the child.

When God Comes

Chapter 17 can be organized in these three sections, dividing the covenant into three parts: God's part, Abram's part and Sarai's part.[7]

---

[5] McLellan, 76.

[6] Quoted by McLellan, 118.

[7] *http://www.jesuswalk.com/abraham/6_circumcision.htm.*

- *God's part* (vv. 3-8)—"As for Me..." Here is God's part of the covenant where He assured Abraham he would have descendants in a Promised Land.
- *Abram's part* (vv. 9-14)—"As for you ... " Abram's part of the covenant is that he must submit to circumcision.
- *Sarai's part* (vv. 15, 16)—"As for Sarai ... " Sarah will bear a son.

In that second encounter, other things happened as well. First, God changed the name[8] of *Abram* to *Abraham*, and He changed the name of *Sarai*, to *Sarah*.[9] The name change was accomplished by the addition of the Hebrew letter *Hay* (similar to *H* in English) to the names. The significance of the change is not

---

[8] The origins of ancient Jewish names go back to the original structure of Jewish society. Ancient Jewish society was structured into **three societal groups**. The top level was that of the **tribe** (*mateh* or *shebet*) ruled by a patriarchal ancestor (later a judge and later still an elected king) and the priesthood in matters that were in their purview. Below that came the extended family or **clan** (*mishpacha* or *aloof*) governed by the elders (*zekenim*) or leaders (*aloofim*). This was made up of related families within the tribe. The third level was the group living within the same **tent** (*ohel*) or house (*bayit*)—what we would call today the **family unit**. Abram was the head of a clan. But he was about to become the father not of a tribe, but of a cluster of tribes—a multitude (*http://www. jewishgen.org/SefardSIG/-yohasin.HTM*).

[9] Abram meant "exalted father." Abraham meant "father of a multitude." The name Sarai meant "princess," and Sarah meant "princess of all." There is no critical, essential difference between the change of either of the two names. The significance was the fusion of the last letter in YHWH into both their names.

the slight change in meaning. The Hebrew letter *Hay* is the last letter in God's distinctive Hebrew name, "YHW<u>H</u>." The addition of the letter *H* indicates a new relationship with God. They now shared the name of God as a wife who takes the name of her husband and shares his identity, his life and fortunes, in a new relationship. This name change was a defining moment in their lives. It redefined who they were. More importantly, it declared who they would become.[10] Yahweh took them into His family.

Second, He ordered that Abraham be circumcised with all his house (vv. 11-13). Abraham immediately complied. And finally, He specifically reaffirmed the promise of a son: "Sarah your wife shall bear you a son" (v. 19).

A Feast for Angels

Now, the Angel of the Lord was back a third time. Abraham cried out to Sarah to make fresh bread. The morning biscuits would not do. What Sarah cooked up is the equivalent of 20 loaves of bread. Abraham ran to pick out fresh meat for the meal. An ordinary meal, even for a wealthy sheik, would consist of flour, along with some camel's milk, boiled together and offered as cakes. Sweet milk and rice would be an extraordinary offering of hospitality.[11] The cakes described here, baked in the fires of a hot hearthstone, were a delicacy (1 Kings 19:6).

[10] *http://www.orthohelp.com/geneal/differ.HTM.*
[11] Charles John Ellicott, *Ellicott's Commentary on the Whole Bible,* Vol. I (Grand Rapids: Zondervan, 1954) 74.

The amount of food is staggering; the variety is festive; the menu is broad enough for royalty. The offering of any meat would have been rare, but Abraham did not merely offer a piece of meat. He did not prepare a quarter or a side, but a whole beef,[12] some say a lamb. Three *measures,* or 3 *seahs,* was about 2 gallons. Butter (*chemah*) here is curdled milk[13] — a treat. The cheese was probably made of cow's milk. The fresh milk would have been from the camels, and the sour milk, also a treat, from the sheep. This was not an offering of leftovers; this was his best. He would trust no one else to determine the portions of the preparation and the quality of service. He offered his freshest. He prepared a veritable feast. It was his personal gift—noble courtesy.[14]

He would spread the gourmet meal out under the shade of the oak trees. And while it was being prepared, he would wash the feet of angels. Extraordinary. One angel, you will recall, is no mere angel. Abraham was washing the feet of God.

Normally, this would have been the task of a servant. It would have been enough to have provided the water necessary for the travelers to wash their own feet, but not on this occasion. Abraham would find no higher role in his life than to kneel before God manifested in physical form and serve Him. This is worship—to be at the feet of God, to touch

---

[12] Victor H. Matthews, Manners and Customs of the Bible (Peabody: Hendrickson, 1988) 19.

[13] James M. Freeman, *Manners and Customs of the Bible* (Springdale, PA: Whitaker, 1996) 19.

[14] Ellicott, 74.

Him, to refresh Him, to bow before Him, to wash the dirt and dust of this world from the Lord. It is in serving God that we are exalted. It is in bowing before Him that we are lifted up. Nothing is more becoming than man kneeling at the feet of Jesus.

After the meal was prepared, Abraham himself would serve it. But he would not presume to sit with the heavenly visitors. This was not a meal *with* God, but a meal *for* God. Abraham would stand like a servant, attending to their every need. "What do you want? Is it prepared to your liking? Do you want something else? What about more butter for your bread?" He was exuberant to serve. His whole focus was on pleasing his guests.

In both the Tabernacle and later the Temple, the altar was known as the table of the Lord. Yet, God declares, "If I were hungry I would not tell you, for the world is mine, and all that is in it" (Psalm 50:12, *NIV*). Neither God nor angels need physical food. God feeds from our love. He does not need it, but He desires it. God is not moved into relationship with us as we are with Him. Without Him, we would perish. We can't live without Him anymore than we can live without air. Our need drives us to Him. He, on the other hand, is moved toward us by His own pure love. He does not need us, but He loves to love us. And somehow, our love feeds Him.

The Fellowship of the Holy

Love is dynamic. It requires an object other than

itself. Love functions as a dynamic verb, not a static noun. The three persons of our Christian Trinity—Father, Son and Holy Spirit—experience perfect love. They are bound together in such a perfect union of love, they are one! "The Father loves the Son" (John 3:35; 5:20; 10:17). Within the relationship of Father, Son and Spirit, there is perfect love—three persons who love one another unconditionally. There is enough love in them and between them for the whole universe, and they have invited us into their fellowship.

If God were not a Trinity, to express and experience love, He would *need* others to love. And He would *need* others outside Himself who would love Him. Love requires another. From the love of the Trinity at the center of the universe flows life itself. It is a fountain that serves to flood the whole of the universe with *agape*. It is this love that empowers our love, making us capable of self-giving love toward others.

Neil Anderson says the following:

> Our heavenly Father didn't need us, but He wants us. This unconditional love and acceptance of God is the essential foundation for our holy living....There are no illegitimate children of God, none of us were unwanted or unexpected accidents....We are not castoffs in an orphanage acting on our best behavior so someone might adopt us. Titus 3:4, 5 tells us, "But when the kindness and love of God our Savior appeared, he saved us, not because of righteous things we had done, but because of his mercy" (*NIV*).[15]

---

[15] Neil Anderson, *Who I Am in Christ* (Ventura, CA: Regal, 1993, 2001) 77.

Prayer is the means by which we are invited into the fellowship of the Trinity. And by prayer, God opens a doorway in us through which He loves our broken world.

Hosting His Presence

It was always God's desire to be present on the earth. Creation still bears His fingerprints. The heavens declare the glory of God, and the earth shows His handiwork. But man was created in His image. And beyond that, God created man's body as a dwelling place. He breathed into man, and man became a living soul. Man's body was of the earth, but his soul had a divine spark, and his spirit was from heaven. He gave God visibility in the earth. He was the regent of God among all other creatures. His heart was God's favorite home in the earth.

When Adam and Eve sinned, God was exiled from the heart of man. The exile of God has escalated. Whole nations reject Him; cities ignore Him; legislatures rule against Him; courts forbid the mention of His name; whole people groups are without His presence. In time, God himself would visit the earth in Christ, only to be soundly rejected by mankind—crucified. In the midst of this rejection, God looks for a man to entertain Him in the earth, to host Him, to celebrate His presence on and in the earth. In the Jewish people, He finds a nation that He can call His people. In Israel, He finds a land to which He can attach His promises. In the Tabernacle and later

67

the Temple, He finds a building in which He can dwell. In Abraham, He finds the man who will host Him in the earth.

God is still looking for those who will entertain Him. At the end of the letters to the seven churches, Christ himself is standing outside knocking, asking for the invitation to reenter (Revelation 3:20). He wants someone—a man, a family, a church, a people, a company—to entertain Him.

This was certainly not the first day Abraham had sat in his tent door watching sojourners travel the water-parting route. This was probably not the first time he had offered hospitality. But this day would be different from all the others, and this trio of travelers would change his life. There is no better picture of prayer in all of Scripture than the one before us. Abraham is entertaining God. And entertaining God is the essence of prayer. We think prayer is petition—presenting our needs to God, or talking to God. No, it is deeper. It is beyond words, beyond communication. Prayer is hosting God.

Entertaining God is not wordy praying. It is serving His presence. It is making a home for God in the earth. It is declaring His right to be in a world that first ignored Him, and then sought to banish Him. He came here, in the flesh, and our world crucified Him. We tend to think that the world is open to His presence. It is not. It kills the prophets, persecutes His disciples, rejects His government, disdains His principles and breaks His laws (Matthew 23:37). He is

68

looking for those who will host Him in a world that is hostile to Him and His kingdom. Could that be you? *oh yea!* Is that why you are now at your new work station? Transferred to a new unit? In a new neighborhood?

Kneeling before Him wordless or lying prostrate at the start of the day, we declare, "This day is Yours! Use it for Your glory. I am Your servant today. What do You need? How can I serve You?" Such daily discipline may not be fraught with "God moments." There may not be smoke and fire, but the practice of regular times of *discipline* is certain to lead to more frequent moments of *delight*—times when God's unmistakable presence comes pouring in around you. The connection between these two is unpredictable and simultaneously undeniable.

The Asian Research Center in Manila surveyed 800 missionaries and discovered that their primary spiritual struggle was in sustaining a consistent personal prayer time. No other problem came close in the minds of the missionaries.[16]

William Temple reminds us, "When I pray, coincidences happen, and when I don't, they don't."[17]

---

[16] Bill Thrasher, *A Journey to Victorious Praying* (Chicago: Moody, 2003) 107.
[17] Quoted by McLellan, 192.

4

THE WORLD'S DISREGARD
FOR GOD

The earth is the Lord's! It is twice His. He created it. Evidence for His creation abounds everywhere. It is not within the scope of this book to defend creationism. Wonderful books can be found in abundance that accomplish that goal. Suffice it to say, the denial of the creative claim of God on the earth is one of the first steps toward apostasy and judgment. Paul says, "The wrath of God is revealed ... against all ungodliness and unrighteousness of men" (Romans 1:18).

Without the Creator, you and I are cosmic orphans. We are the children of the earth and its heavens, a step away from paganism. The moral implications of evolution are staggering.

1. It is the embrace of change as a philosophy of life.

2. It feeds existentialism.
3. It nurtures nihilism.
4. It makes a bleep on the radar screen of time with no history and no destiny.

We came from nowhere, and we have nowhere to go. We are now identified, not as created in the image of God, as bearing something divine within our souls, but with the lower animal kingdom. Rather than having God as our Father, we are the products of random chance, alone in the vast universe.

People arrive at such an intellectual position only because they "suppress the truth in unrighteousness" (v. 18). Paul says such men know "what may be known of God." It "is manifest in them, for God has shown it to them" (v. 19). It is evident in "the creation of the world." God's "invisible attributes are clearly seen, being understood by the things that are made, even His eternal power and Godhead" (v. 20).

The earth is "without excuse" (v. 20). The deliberate decision to suppress truth not only sets the earth up for judgment, it changes man on the inside. It blinds him. It hardens him. It places him on a downward moral slide. "They knew God, [but] they did not glorify Him as God" (v. 21). They do not withhold worship altogether; they redirect it. They actually worship themselves.

Isaiah would call it a heart problem: "They draw near with their lips, but their heart is far from Me!" (see 29:13). They retain the language of faith, but they have lost faith in their hearts. Deep reverence for God is lost. Faith is optional. Morality is relative. An objective, sobering and shaking encounter with the sovereign God is something now lost. Israel's God was no longer held as utterly unique and incomparable among the gods of the nations. What a compelling description of our era.

Paul says that such thinking gives birth to an insensitive and carnal culture. It is characterized by a lack of gratitude. People then become "futile in their thoughts" (Romans 1:21), trapped in logical systems loaded with flawed reason. They have omitted God from all their formulas. Then something more devastating than mere mental error occurs — their "foolish hearts were darkened" (v. 21). The inner moral lights now go out. "Professing to be wise, they became fools" (v. 22). They now have a perverted perception of God — "[changing] the glory of the incorruptible God into an image made like corruptible man" (v. 23).

Isaiah would declare, "They turn everything upside down. How silly they are to think that potters are like the clay they work with! Can what is made say to the one who made it, 'You didn't make me'? Can the pot say to the potter, 'You don't know anything'?" (see 29:16). They think God is like them . . . that they know as much as He does. His treasures of knowledge are cast away by these people. Rejecting the record of His self-disclosure, they use themselves as a starting point for spiritual discovery. They grope like drunk, blind men. Isaiah foresaw them. They would "pause and wonder" as if confused, lost, uncertain (v. 9),

73

saying, "Who sees us? . . . Who knows us?" (v. 15). "Blind yourselves and be blind!" the prophet would cry out (v. 9). Having lost sight of the true God, they first slip into idolatry and then into deep immorality. "God also gave them up to uncleanness . . . who exchanged the truth of God for the lie, and worshiped and served the creature rather than the Creator" (Romans 1:24, 25). Having lost God, they have also lost their moral reference points. Being blind to this glorious Creator, they now only see the creature. Having rejected truth, they are like surveyors whose reference point is wrong, explorers who journey stubbornly forward with a defective compass. They are lost leaders. Their premise for discovery is based on a lie!

God created this world. It belongs to Him, as does man himself.

> The earth is the Lord's, and all its fullness, the world and those who dwell therein. For He has founded it upon the seas, and established it upon the waters (Psalm 24:1, 2).

Not only does He have a creative claim on the earth, He also has a redemptive claim. Under the power of sin and death, the earth was illegally seized by Satan, who longs to be known as the "god of this world" (2 Corinthians 4:4, KJV). He dares to presume that the kingdoms of this world are his to give, and did so in the face of Christ on the mount of Temptation (Matthew 4:8, 9). Such a claim is spurious. It is a lie. The earth belongs to the Lord (Exodus 9:29).

74

The earth is twice His—by creation and then redemption. And yet, on this earth the claim of God and the rule of His benevolent kingdom are disputed. In such an hour, God looks to those who will host Him, entertain Him. He wants His followers to launch a prayerful protest that insists on His being honored, that pleads for His in-breaking kingdom, that whispers, "Come quickly, Lord Jesus!" (see Revelation 22:20).

In Revelation 1, Jesus stands in the midst of the churches. His eyes are like lasers. His hair is as white as wool. His robe is glistening. Out of his mouth is a sharp two-edged sword. His words cut. They slice. You are defenseless before Him. He holds you and me by the mere power of His speech. One word would fell us. One accusation against us—and we are dead. You are mesmerized; frozen. You have never encountered power in a person like this before. His face is like the noonday sun. You cannot gaze at it. You glance and shield your eyes. The power of the encounter is overwhelming. His feet appear as a reddish-orange, as if He has gone through a live lava flow and they are still aglow, but He is unmoved, unaffected by what He has just endured.

No creature Hollywood has ever imagined could be more disabling, more paralyzing, than an encounter with the resurrected, ascended, enthroned and glorified Christ. John collapses before Him. He faints like a dead man (v. 17). He had once clung to Jesus in a fashion more familiar than any other disciple (John

13:23). No more. Now he finds Him unapproachable.

The world's last glimpse of Him is as a helpless victim on the cross—the crucified Jesus. This should not be the prevailing view with the church, but it is. Having forgotten who it is that we worship—the resurrected, ascended Lord of Glory—we treat Him as the powerless Galilean. Liberal theologians strip Him of the record of the miraculous and make Him only a man who is slightly more insightful than they are. Our world fashions Him as a bit more sensitive than we are ourselves; perhaps less. And having made Him like ourselves, we too expel Him from our church.

So in Revelation 3, at the end of the church age, He stands outside, knocking on the door of the church itself, longing to be entertained by His own bride, received by His own people. He forever comes to His own, who receive Him not (John 1:11).

From Omnipresence to Glory

Some argue that Christ does not need to be entertained, that His presence does not need to be invited. It is true that God is everywhere (Psalm 139:7-12). David declared, "If I make my bed in hell ... You are there!" (v. 8). This is called the *omnipresence of God*. So pervasive is the reach of God, that there is no place where He is not. Some attempt to imagine in what part of this universe God might reside. In truth, God is not in the universe; the universe is in His embrace.

Beyond Omnipresence to His Abiding Presence

This spatial and cosmic permeation of the presence of God is not the personal God for whom we long. There is another dimension of God's presence. He promises to His followers, "Lo, I am with you always" (Matthew 28:20). He will never leave us or forsake us (Hebrews 13:5). This is the *abiding presence of God*. When we walk through the valley of the shadow of death, He is there (Psalm 23). When we lie down by still waters or stand face-to-face with enemies, He is with us. But we do not always sense His abiding presence.

Walter Brueggemann has suggested that certain psalms can be understood in the categories of order, disorder and the new order:[1]

1. *Psalms of order (orientation)*. All is well. God is near. Victory is assured.

2. *Psalms of disorder (disorientation)*. Our world is in some way turned upside down. We are surprised by tragedy. God and His promises seem to vanish. We cry, but there is no answer. We plead, but there is no immediate deliverer.

3. *Psalms of the new order (reorientation)*. The disorder

[1] Walter Brueggemann, *The Message of the Psalms* (Minneapolis: Augsburg, 1984) 11, 21-3.

is past. We have navigated through the turbulent waters. Our boat has not capsized. We are in a new season. We move from order, through disorder, to a new order; from a positive orientation, into a season of disorientation, and then onward to reorientation. And when that new order is like an old shoe, or perhaps before we break it in, we are again in disorder. Disorder is not a destination, but a place of transition. We move through it. We sometimes misguidedly hope to recover the old order. But we can never go back, we can only go forward to a new order. This is how God grows us. In the seasons of disorder, God is no less present. But we may not sense His presence. Still, He abides.

Beyond His Abiding Presence to the Quickened Presence

What most of us long for is His felt presence. We want to experience Him. We long to have a *quickened sense of God's presence*. No one has to tell genuine Christians when they are experiencing the presence of God. All God's kids know His presence—Pentecostals and liturgicals, Calvinists and Arminians, rich and poor, every race. God is everywhere. He is *omnipresent*. But His Spirit lives in His kids—this is His abiding presence. But there are moments when all alone we experience the reality of the presence of God. This is the *quickened sense* of God's presence. But there is more.

His Dynamic Presence

Jesus said, "Where two or three are gathered together in My name, I am there in the midst of them" (Matthew 18:20). As living stones of a lively temple, when we come together, we give place to another dimension of God's presence—*His dynamic presence* (1 Peter 2:5). Suddenly, the "two or three" of us, or 200 to 300 of us, are experiencing the presence of God together, simultaneously. And we all know it.

His Manifest Presence

There is yet another dimension to God's presence. It is the *manifest presence of God*. At such times, God becomes so real that our physical senses register His presence. He manifests Himself to us. Abraham saw Him . . . touched Him . . . heard Him. Israel followed a cloud by day and a pillar of fire by night. Moses experienced a burning bush. Elijah saw fire fall from heaven.

God is real—and at *kairos* (opportune) times, He breaks into our world in ways that are undeniable. This is *the manifest presence of God*.

Anne Graham Lotz is the daughter of Billy and Ruth Graham. Her books bear the mark of a passion for Jesus that is rare and extraordinary. Her ministry seems to flow out of her love relationship with God. She recalls that as a child her room was above that of her mom and dad. When her father was away, she would look for opportunities to sneak down to catch a private moment with her mother before

79

bedtime. She could see the light in her mother's room reflected on the lawn of their mountain house. But more often than not, when she crept down to steal a few private moments, she would crack the bedroom door only to find Ruth Graham on her knees in prayer. She comments, "It was useless to wait for her to rise because she would be there for hours on end." In the morning, the lights would be on again in the predawn hours. Tumbling down the stairs, she would find her mother at her desk, "earnestly reading and studying one of 14 translations of the Bible she had spread out around her."[2]

It is God's desire that we entertain Him. He can kick in the doors of our lives, our churches and our cities. He will not be shut out when He, the Sovereign God, decides to enter. But the result of His forcible entry often means judgment.

You and I are called to entertain Him at work, at home, in our neighborhoods—everywhere we go. We are living tabernacles. We are to be mobile units for the divine presence. By living in us, He dwells in the earth. By honoring Him in quiet, yet passionate worship, we engage Him on His throne. By obedient cooperation, His presence not only resides in our fleshly temples, He radiates through us to a world enshrouded in darkness. That changes our lives. It marks our homes. Entertaining God shapes our children.

---

[2] Anne Graham Lotz, *My Heart's Cry* (Nashville: Word, 2002) 148.

We should not rest until 24/7 deliberate and intentional prayer is established in every major geographic center on the earth; until we have identified prayer centers and mobilized intercessors to pray for the nations that now live in our cities. We should not rest until there are intercessors on the walls in every city, day and night, crying out for revival and renewal. Every corner and quarter of the city should be covered by prayer. We should not rest until every high-rise building, every apartment complex, every school and government office, every prison and place of pain, every corporate office and service agency—is covered by a prayer team.

MOVEMENT TWO

Entertaining God
Breaks the Barrenness

Genesis 18:9-15

Then they said to him, "Where is Sarah your wife?"

So he said, "Here, in the tent."

And He said, "I will certainly return to you according to the time of life, and behold, Sarah your wife shall have a son."

(Sarah was listening in the tent door which was behind him.) Now Abraham and Sarah were old, well advanced in age; and Sarah had passed the age of childbearing. Therefore Sarah laughed within herself, saying, "After I have grown old, shall I have pleasure, my lord being old also?"

And the Lord said to Abraham, "Why did Sarah laugh, saying, 'Shall I surely bear a child, since I am old?' Is anything too hard for the Lord? At the appointed time I will return to you, according to the time of life, and Sarah shall have a son."

But Sarah denied it, saying, "I did not laugh," for she was afraid.

And He said, "No, but you did laugh!"

When Work for God Is More Important Than Worship of God

When Alan Redpath was the pastor of the great Moody Bible Church, he was at the peak of ministry opportunities. His church was in a season of explosive growth. National conferences longed for his participation. At what seemed like the pinnacle of his career, his daughter found him facedown in his study, incapable of movement—the victim of a massive stroke. His career seemed over.

He was completely immobilized, but utterly alert. He could not lift his head, move his feet, or raise his hand. He could not open his mouth. For three months that seemed like years, he prayed and searched his heart for the "why?" of it all. He was certain that Satan had succeeded in stopping his successful ministry. And he was equally determined to wait it out, to win a victory, to recover, and give a solid blow to the kingdom of darkness. But he was in for a surprise.

Propped up in his bed, three months into the ordeal, his eye fell on his open Bible on the table at his bedside. Shocking words leaped off the page: "Remove thy stroke away from me: I am consumed by the blow of thine hand" (Psalm 39:10, KJV).

Incredible. Impossible. The stroke was from the hand of God? The shock of the moment was stunning. God had stopped him?

God had paralyzed him? In that moment, intuitively he knew why.

His work for God had taken precedence over his worship of God. He repented. No stalling. No rationalizing. Immediately he could speak. In that moment, the powerful hold of his stroke was broken.

He returned to active and productive ministry, vowing never again to allow his personal relationship with God to have a secondary role to his business relationship in behalf of Christ.[1]

---

[1] Anne Graham Lotz, *My Heart's Cry* (Nashville: Word, 2002) 130.

5

BREAKING THE
BARRENNESS!

A braham and Sarah were childless. Sarah was barren. She had gone through the change of life and was beyond menopause. There would be no children. It was physically impossible for both of them. More than a decade before this moment, the Scriptures report that she had passed the age of childbearing (Genesis 16:2). And Abraham too felt he was past the age of fertility (17:17). They were "stricken in age" (18:11, KJV).[1] Sarah would ask, "Children? After I am waxed old shall I have pleasure?" (see v. 12). The Hebrew word for *waxed old* means to be "worn out like an old garment."[2] And the word for *pleasure* is the Hebrew *'ednah*, with

---

[1] Brian L. Harbour, *Famous Couples of the Bible* (Nashville: Broadman, 1979) 23.
[2] Harbour, 75.

echoes of Eden, the fruitful Garden of Genesis.[3] Sarah was now confronted with a God who could bring newness into the most final of human endings. God's time is not our time. He uses wasted people, impossible scenarios. He chooses the long odds.

Marriage Fractures

Physical problems were not the only challenges of this couple. They had relationship problems. "Their marriage revolved around the child they had not been able to have, the child God had promised but had not delivered."[4] Life that is centered around an empty cradle can be full of pain—an unfinished dream, a hope not yet realized that wouldn't go away. Abraham could not release himself from the impossible dream. Finally, the dream turned into a nightmare. Hagar had been a wonderful handmaiden to Sarah. But empowered by moments of intimacy in the embrace of Abraham, she had turned into another woman. And so had Sarah: "I gave my maid into your embrace; and when she saw that she had conceived, I became despised in her eyes" (Genesis 16:5). The triangle threatened to destroy the relationship. Sarah was livid. Hagar had to go, and so did the boy! This was Abraham's boy, his son.

---

[3] J. Gerald Janzen, *Abraham and All the Families of the Earth: International Theological Commentary* (Grand Rapids: Eerdmans, 1993) 55.

[4] Harbour, 24.

James Dobson reminds us, "Pain and suffering do not cause the greatest damage in times of trial. Confusion is the factor that shreds one's faith."[5] When affairs happen in marriage, it shatters confidence and trust. It threatens the permanency of the relationship. Another door has been opened. Another option has been created. One shoe has dropped: when will the other fall? It introduces the possibility of abandonment to the other spouse and to the children.

Sarah despised Hagar. Her trusted friend, even as a subordinate, was now a bitter enemy. Sarah had now become a victim. Hagar felt empowered. She had slept with Abraham and had replaced, at least for a moment, Sarah. She now had something with which she could barter, something Abraham wanted that Sarah could not give—a son. In that not-so-small way, she felt superior. Her attitude toward Sarah changed. She no longer ran when Sarah rang the call bell. She now lingered in Abraham's presence. No doubt Abraham cared because she was bearing his child. "Sit here, out of the sun. Come into the tent. Lie down. Sarah won't mind. Sarah, would you get Hagar some. . . ? " He wouldn't have dared! Sarah did mind! Sarah had been displaced, dishonored. And she blamed Abraham: "My wrong be upon you!" (16:5). The conflict became so intense that Hagar fled. The Angel of the Lord himself advised Hagar to return and change her own attitude toward

---

[5] Quoted by Vernon McLellan, *Thoughts That Shaped the Church* (Wheaton: Tyndale, 2000) 234.

Sarah: "Submit yourself under her hand" (v. 9). Pregnant, Hagar returned. Eventually, she gave birth to a son.

What had they done? It had seemed right. But oh, how wrong it felt now! Triangles never work. Unfaithfulness may momentarily taste sweet, but it swallows sour.

Dashed Dreams

They had psychological stresses to deal with. Abraham had left Haran (12:1) with bright hope. God would make of him a great nation. In 12:7 and 15:4, 5, God reaffirmed the message.[6] Ten years later, there was no promised child. Abraham and Sarah were still in a strange land with a nomadic life and an empty bassinet. How long can you live on hope? Now they were aging, with no children to care for them, no social security for old age.

Something happens in midlife. You begin to count, not the years you have lived, but the years you have left to live. Abraham and Sarah were well beyond midlife and something had to be done. Time was slipping away. Enter Hagar! Problem "solved." But their tinkering with divine promises only complicated matters, almost destroying their marriage. Now, 13 additional years have gone by since Abraham had even heard from God. Had He given up on them? Did He blow the promise away with their scheming plot? Was it over? The mystique disappeared. Someone cynically said, "No man is a hero to his wife!"[7]

---

[6] Harbour, 26.

They had seen the worst side of the other too many times. They were past trying.

John Hyde was burdened for a pastor in India. He entered into prayer in behalf of the pastor. His prayers immediately focused on the spiritual indifference and coldness of the pastor. He had become a hindrance instead of a help to God's work. But God surprised John Hyde. Instead of acceding to the opinion John expressed in prayer, God put his finger on the heart of John himself. God revealed the critical spirit in which he was praying. John saw that he was agreeing with "the accuser of the brethren" (Revelation 12:10) and not the Holy Spirit. The difference between a condemning spirit and gentle conviction is even missed by veteran intercessors. With God the line is not so slight; it is the difference between two poles. Instead of focusing on the pastor's indifference, John asked God to show him things for which he could praise the pastor at the throne of heaven in prayer. He turned his praying on its head and began to genuinely thank God for the pastor, asking for grace to work in his life, for God to intervene, for the favor and blessing of God. As he began to intercede in this different way, the pastor experienced a personal revival. His heart was changed. Attitudes and actions soon revealed this remarkable change.[8]

read all - very good

---

[7] Harbour, 26.

[8] Bill Thrasher, *A Journey to Victorious Praying* (Chicago: Moody, 2003) 45.

Max Lucado says:

> Weariness is tough. I don't mean the physical
> weariness that comes from mowing the lawn
> or the mental weariness that follows a hard day
> of decisions and thinking. . . . It's the weariness
> that comes just before you give up. That feeling
> of honest desperation. It's the dispirited father,
> the abandoned child, or the retiree with time on
> his hands. It's that stage in life when motiva-
> tion disappears: the children grow up, a job is
> lost, a wife dies. The result is weariness—deep,
> lonely, frustrated weariness. Only one man in
> history has claimed to have an answer for it.
> He stands before all the weary sufferers of the
> world with the same promise, "Come to me,
> all you who are weary. . . and I will give you
> rest" (Matthew 11:28, *NIV*).[9]

For 24 years, Abraham and Sarah had carried
around a promise. And for 24 years, it had been
unfulfilled. Whatever God conceives supernaturally
has to be gestated and delivered supernaturally. You
cannot grasp a supernatural promise and fulfill it
in a natural way. They tried . . . they failed. Many
have received a "word from the Lord" and worked
feverishly to bring it to pass. Such an approach is
futile. If it is conceived by the Spirit, it must be birthed
by the Spirit. If in entertaining God, He gives the
vision, then only by prayerfully entertaining God
will the vision become reality.

---

[9] Quoted by McLellan, 233-4.

J.B. Phillips reminds us: *Vny Book.*

Life is full of people who "used to believe." But because things turned out darker and tougher than they supposed, they had decided that "there can't be a God to let things like that happen." But "things like that" have always happened, to all sorts of people; even to Christ. We simply do not know why life should, apparently, be so easy for one and so heart-breakingly difficult for another. Let's not pretend. No one likes pain or difficulty or this sense of darkness and being alone. But if we can accept it as a part of life and hold on to the God who, apparently, isn't there, we shall eventually emerge toughened and strengthened.[10]

Impatience Produces Ishmael

Abraham did not always patiently wait. He and Sarah both experienced a crisis of their faith. He went to God to substitute Eliezer's line as the promise. God said, "No!" Sarah then came to him and suggested that Hagar be her substitute. To that, Abraham readily agreed. That substitution has been Israel's nightmare.

Sometimes the vision God gives us is so impossible, so extraordinary, that we cannot believe it. So we trim it back, and substitute a doable thing for the impossible mission to which God has called us. The result is almost always disastrous. E. Stanley Jones says, "Some people go through life getting results; others getting consequences."[11] Hagar and Sarah are

---

[10] Quoted by McLellan, 234.
[11] Quoted by McLellan, 150.

still fighting today. Ishmael and Isaac both claim the land of Abraham. It is the hot spot of global politics.

Stand outside that tent and counsel Abraham. Tell him, "What you are about to do will haunt your children. You cannot make the things of the Spirit come to pass by the actions of flesh. What God wants to do, He wants to do with you and your spouse within the context of that covenant. Don't go into that tent! The whole world is out here watching you. This is no private moment. Trust God. Wait. God will, in time, bring you and Sarah to a place of unity on this."

Keep coaching him. Get tough with him: "You are not only giving up on Sarah, you are giving up on God! Abraham, may I say to you, my dear brother, that you are intoxicated by a view of yourself that is superior to Sarah. You are about to consort with her handmaiden. Does she believe in the promise more than Sarah? You cannot make this substitution. You cannot allow a bond with this woman in the place of your wife. No! God will bring Sarah to a place of faith. She will believe. She will bear the son you long for. Abraham, don't go into that tent!"

But he did. And so have we at times. We enter the tent with Hagar when we scheme to accomplish a noble God-given vision. We enter the tent when we partner in dubious ways. In the embrace of Hagar, we find ourselves compromised. The result is always the same—regret, consequences, negative generational impact. It is a stain on our character, a mark on our record.

And yet, when such compromises come, God's grace works still. Abraham and Sarah were not perfect, but in them and through them, God's grace worked perfectly. Charles E. Cowman reminds us:

> Circumstances may appear to wreck our lives and God's plans, but God is not helpless among the ruins. Our broken lives are not lost or useless. God's love is still working. He comes in and takes the calamity and uses it victoriously, working out His wonderful plan of love.[12]

---

[12] Quoted by McLellan, 114.

6

GOD'S PERFECT TIMING—
A FATHER AT 100

It is laughable, isn't it? God's ways are downright hilarious. Imagine a 75-year-old man with his 65-year-old wife showing up in your congregation with the testimony:

> Pastor, we are new to the area. We just moved down here from the north, and we are on a mission, a spiritual mission. You see, we have never been able to have children, but God told us to move here and He was going to give us so many children they would be like the sand on the sea and stars in the heavens.
>
> We're buying baby furniture this week and painting the nursery. If any of the members want to come over and help us, we'd welcome them. By the way, we're taking donations of baby clothes and toys. It's gonna be a boy!
>
> Pray for us, Preacher.

"Like the sand of the sea and the stars of the heavens," the words of the old man's testimony echo. There is laughter. It is a cute testimony. Sweet, but utterly ridiculous. The next Sunday comes along, and the old man and his wife are back.

> Preacher, could I say a word? Some folks mis-understood me last time. I was serious. I believe God has told me that Sarai and I are going to have children. Preacher, would you and the elders here agree with me for this promise?

Could you agree with that old man? Honestly? Believe with him? Encourage him in this dream? How long would it be before he had worn the congregation out repeating his faith in the impossible vision? Given the atmosphere of most churches, Abram and Sarai would have been forced into isolation simply to survive. The preacher would have been told, "Don't let that old man testify anymore about the sand and the stars! It's an embarrassment."

Month after month and year after year, two decades pass. Could you hold on to an impossible word from the Lord for that long?

- This is the faith legacy of the aged Caleb, who, at 80 years old, had outlived a doubting generation to claim a mountain full of giants and drive them out.
- This is the company of Joshua, who was only one of two who had lived to see both the Red Sea part and the Jordan roll back. An old man, a skilled warrior, he would lead an incredible

military conquest and oversee the settlement of the Promised Land.

- This is the heritage of Moses, who found his purpose at the age of 80, and peered into the Promised Land at the age of 120.
- This is the circle of Anna, 84 years old, who had lived in the Temple for years in anticipation of the Messiah (Luke 2:37). She saw Him, she held Him, and blessed Him.
- This is the story of Zacharias and Elizabeth, too old for children. While Zacharias was praying in the Temple, burning incense at the time of prayer—entertaining God—the barrenness of his wife was broken.

From that couple comes the prophetic ministry of John the Baptist (1:13). You are never too old to fulfill your destiny. *Today 2•20 I am almost 82 yes. ald. 2 agree! Look out devil.*

Discovering Spring in Winter

For more than two decades, Abraham held his promise, even if Sarah had not held it with the same passion. In part, the mission of the Angel of the Lord was to bring Sarah and Abraham into a place of unifying faith. This was about the home and the recovery of faith in a 25-year-old vision. It was about unfinished business and unfulfilled promises. It was about a servant nation that would bless the world. It was about the family, the fountainhead of God's grace to the earth that cannot be underestimated.

What "a comfort to drop the tangles of life into God's hands and leave them there," Mrs. Charles E. Cowman reminds us.[1] This longing of Abraham reaches beyond a desire for a son with whom he might go for a camel ride. He longed for his lineage to be a source of blessing to the earth.

What do we teach our children about their purpose on the earth? That they are here for themselves? Or that they are to be catalysts for positive change in culture, a vehicle for the grace and truth of God, a conduit of blessing through which God touches all those around them?

Here is destiny, purpose, personal mission—all of these things ride on the back of Abraham's longing for "stars and sand."

Abraham and Sarah consigned themselves to the stable, ordinary run of life, but out of that came only hopelessness and despair. It had been 13 years since Abraham had heard from God—13 years, since his liaison with Hagar had produced Ishmael. They were years of deafening silence. Now there were two back-to-back visits (Genesis 17; 18). Yahweh had ordered the change of Abram's name to *Abraham* and also mandated circumcision. Abraham had complied. Suddenly, Yahweh was back for the second unannounced visit with fresh hope. The couple would have a son. Abraham had done his part. Now God would do His part, enabling Sarah to do hers.

[1] Quoted by Vernon McLellan, *Thoughts That Shaped the Church* (Wheaton: Tyndale, 2000) 114.

When God Confronts

The Angel of the Lord inquired, "Where is Sarah your wife?" (18:9). Such an inquiry was contrary to the manners of the region. Women were referred to only indirectly. The Angel violated the cultural rules. He knew Sarah's location. She was in the tent behind the woman's partition.[2] What He said was for her hearing. One of the purposes of His visit was to say, "Sarah will have a child!" She was listening to the dialogue as all good wives would have done.

In the first movement of the passage, Sarah was the auxiliary, and Abraham offered hospitality to the angels. Now, Abraham is the auxiliary, and it is Sarah who is the focus of the angelic dialogue. In the first movement, Abraham was invited to be a host. Now, Sarah was about to be told that her body will host the divine promise: she will have son.[3]

She laughed at the idea—within herself. Bernard Ramm declared, "Humor reminds us that we are not gods and goddesses."[4] Sarah dismissed the message of the angels as fanciful. It was not something she was opposed to, but it was something impossible. But hope is the oxygen of the soul. We can't live without it![5] *If we lose it we die. message on hope*

[2] James M. Freeman, *Manners and Customs of the Bible* (Springdale, PA: Whitaker, 1996) 19.

[3] J. Gerald Janzen, *Abraham and All the Families of the Earth: International Theological Commentary* (Grand Rapids: Eerdmans, 1993) 57.

[4] Quoted by McLellan, 139.

[5] Chip Ingram, *God—As He Longs for You to See Him* (Grand Rapids: Baker, 2004) 209.

There is so much grace in the confrontation of Sarah by Yahweh. Speaking to her indirectly lessened the embarrassment of her lack of faith. Mediation is sometimes most effective when it is indirect. Addressed to a third party, it "respects one's interior consciousness by not intruding directly upon it."[6] Standing outside the tent, as if speaking to Abraham, the Angel applied indirect pressure to Sarah. He promised Sarah, not Abraham, a son. Abraham claimed the promise, while Sarah was slow to believe.

The private laughter became a matter of public conversation. The Lord would not let her get away with hiding behind such a mask of denial. That mask was ripped away by the simple statement of fact, "Yes, you did laugh" (v. 15, *NIV*). So, the coming child would be called *Isaac*—"laughter."

Sarah didn't sneer in bitterness and anger. She did not seethe with resentment that the subject of her barrenness had arisen with, as far as she knew, complete strangers. She did not appear to suspect Abraham of inappropriate disclosures about her and their relationship. No, she laughed.

Until this moment, this had been an "Abraham" thing. Now the Angel had spoken directly to her. She had bumped into the divine will firsthand, and it changed her. The reality that she could no longer hide her private thoughts frightened her. Her fear came not only from the realization that her private thoughts were revealed, but also for the first time

[6] Janzen, 55

she recognized that she was in a conversation with Yahweh, from which she could not retreat.

Where do you hide when you are in God's presence? He sees through you and me. He reads our minds. He hears words before they are formed or spoken. Her fear came because the laughter was indeed an expression of doubt. And God called that doubt into honest light: "Is anything too hard for the Lord?" (v. 14).

The age issue was not one-sided. "Old as I am . . . and with my husband so old?" (see v. 12). Verse 13 says the Angel of the Lord reported to Abraham only half of the self-conversation of Sarah—only the thoughts about her own age. He said nothing of Sarah's comment about his aging body. Here was grace again. The Talmud says the Angel's report was to spare the couple the opportunity for discord had Abraham known Sarah's true thoughts.[7] After all, the age was only the surface resistance. Lack of faith was the root of Sarah's struggle.

She could deny it no more. It wasn't safe to think contrary thoughts around God. "He knows the thoughts . . . every one of them" (see Job 21:27). The Angel of the Lord challenged Sarah's thinking—she *would* have a child. Nothing is too hard for Yahweh. Sarah had been fixated on the problem—their age. In this moment, God graciously moved her focus from her incapacity to His life-giving capacity. Yahweh

use in message in Hope

---

[7] Adele Berlin, Marc Zvi Brettler and Michael Fishbane, eds., *The Jewish Study Bible* (New York: Oxford UP; the Jewish Publication Society, 2004) 39.

can neither be measured nor contained by our adequacies.[8]

Up Against Impossible

God calls us to the impossible in order that He alone might glory in the results. Our faith is forever— David against Goliath; Daniel against the lions; the three Hebrew boys in the furnace; the Hebrew slaves between the Red Sea and Pharaoh's army. It's Esther against Haman. It's Elijah against a drought and 400 false prophets. It's Moses against the Egyptian Empire; Paul against Nero; Martin Luther against the pope. And, it's Abraham and Sarah against age and the natural order!

Abraham and Sarah, nudged together in faith, realized their vision that the earth will be blessed as a result. Who would have guessed that such destiny resided in the tent of a Bedouin nomad?

This may be the first time Sarah ever really believed the vision for herself. She had doubted the words from the Lord through her husband, Abraham. And she had doubted the words of these angelic visitors. But, somehow, this moment was what she needed to move her to begin to believe! Someone said, "God takes the route that brings Him the most glory! And on its way to better, it may drop by worse."[9]

[8] Janzen, 56.

[9] Ronald Dunn, *Don't Just Stand There, Pray Something: The Incredible Power of Intercessory Prayer* (Nashville: Thomas Nelson, 1992) 203.

Abraham had carried a vision for 24 years, one in which he believed, but one to which his wife was only tolerant. In the beginning, she, too, must have longed for a child. But she was not like the dreamer whom she married. Being more rational and more grounded, she gave up. Let him dream. It was benign. It made him a bit eccentric, but he was a good man.

Abraham might have been tempted at times to confront Sarah, to degrade her for a lack of faith. "If you would only believe, the promise would come true! It's your fault." We find none of that in Scripture. Instead, he carried the unfulfilled promise. "Against hope [he] believed in hope, that he might become the father..." (Romans 4:18, KJV).

Like rose blossoms and butterfly cocoons, some things have to mature in their own time. If you force them open, you damage them. If Abraham had confronted Sarah about her unbelief, he would have placed a wedge in their relationship that would have marred their record. It might have damaged, perhaps destroyed, their relationship. The relationship might have become inflamed. They would have reached a relational impasse. In fact, that might have been the driving force behind the Hagar incident. Then, in an "it's-her-or-me!" moment, Sarah stood toe-to-toe with Abraham.

Abraham must have felt at times that he was trapped between a vision that was so real he could touch it and a wife who, while wonderful and sweet, did not share his passion for the vision. Which does he choose? Does he seek another whose heart is "more in tune with God" to fulfill his vision? Can there be a substitute for Sarah? Does the vision belong only to Abraham? Are a man and a woman, once married, really one? Are their God-given callings and dreams one as well?

In our utilitarian and get-ahead society, we, in the name of God, may see spiritual leaders swap partners "for the glory of God" as they move toward a supposedly God-given vision. But God is not utilitarian. And He will not indiscriminately sacrifice relationships for results.

How many men and women have abandoned their spouses, more married to a vision than to the one to whom God has joined them? Blindly, they believe that a vision given by the same God who joined them together can only be fulfilled if they now abandon their partner in search of one who will make their dream come true and help them fulfill their vision.

If the God who gives the vision is the same as the God who joined you together, He will not be taken by surprise by the struggles you have in jointly coming to terms with the vision. That struggle is as much a part of the process as is the vision itself. The relationship cannot be sacrificed for the reality of the vision. The relationship is critical to the vision.

Martin Marty makes this point:

> Religion and celebrity do not mix. Religion and
> fame might work well together, but celebrity
> is a different matter. The distinction? Try this
> out: Celebrities do not have friends. They are
> surrounded by people, but are actually isolated.
> They have ... people who tell the noted, soon
> to be notorious, cleric what he or she wants to
> hear until each begins to believe the publicity.
> Such friendless clergy take themselves seriously,
> lose perspective, put themselves above the law,
> and invent self-justifying rationales.... What
> are friends for? ... Friends say to people who
> acquire power and position—and even the pas-
> tor of the humble parish has some of that—
> 'Watch it, buddy,' or 'We knew you when....'
> or 'This time you went too far.'"[10]

Don't miss the point. Only by entertaining God,
by inviting Him to our tent, does He do what we
cannot do—open the womb of promise.

David Wilkerson was a young pastor when he
first committed himself to spend an hour a day in
prayer. He was not pouring through commentaries
when it happened. He was leafing through a mag-
azine when he saw the double-page spread telling
the story of the trial involving one of the gangs in
New York City. He was moved so much he attended
the trial. By attempting to get to the kids, he violated
courtroom barriers and created quite a scene. He
was passionate. He had found his calling. He moved

---

[10] Quoted by McLellan, 104.

to the streets of New York to minister to gangs. The result was Teen Challenge ministries around the world. His church in New York is always packed. He has touched the world. It all began by entertaining God.

MOVEMENT THREE

In Entertaining God, He Reveals His Secrets

Genesis 18:16-18

Then the men rose from there and looked toward Sodom, and Abraham went with them to send them on the way. And the Lord said, "Shall I hide from Abraham what I am doing, since Abraham shall surely become a great and mighty nation, and all the nations of the earth shall be blessed in him?"

read with message on hope

A Missionary's Assurance From God in Prayer: Your Children Are Safe!

John and Edith Bell were missionaries in western China. When Japan invaded China in World War II, they were in harm's way. It was a brutal experience. Their children were in Chefoo, some distance from them, in a boarding school with the children of other missionaries. Edith was horrified when she learned that the school had been raided and her three children had been seized and imprisoned at Weihsien Concentration Camp.

Edith turned to prayer—passionate prayer laced with anguish. She cried out to God, begging for His protective care over the children. God whispered to her from His Word— Jeremiah 31:16, 17: "Thus says the Lord: 'Refrain your voice from weeping, and your eyes from tears; for your work shall be rewarded,' says the Lord, 'and they shall come back from the land of the enemy. There is hope in your future,' says the Lord, 'that your children shall come back to their own border.'"

It was such a comforting whisper from the Lord! She claimed it. The Word of the Lord gave her peace, but such moments are rarely given to us without a challenge from the Evil One.

111

Then one day, a man came to her door. He had news from the Weihsien region, and specific news about the children of John and Edith: "They are alive and well cared for. They have adequate food and clothing." What a relief. What a confirmation!

Later, the man returned—this time with a vexing message. "Mrs. Bell, I have some very sad news. All the students in the Weihsien Camp have been murdered."

It was too much! Fear rose to challenge faith. Edith struggled to fend off panic. Her mind reeled. She had the promise of Jeremiah 31:16, 17, given to her in a season of passionate prayer. Retrieving her Chinese Bible, she opened it to the verses and said to the man, "You read this!" He took the Bible; he read the words.

The man threw the Bible to the floor and stormed from the house. Edith was amazed, puzzled. Later, she would learn that the man was an infiltrator whose task was to destroy the morale of Christian leaders remaining in the region. As the war intensified, it became clear that John and Edith could not remain in the country. They had to flee. Traveling westward into India, they escaped and booked passage to America. They were forced to leave their children behind, if their children were even alive. The voyage was fraught with the anxiety of wonder regarding their little ones. When they arrived in New York, they were greeted by a Red Cross worker with unbelievable news—

unbelievable, except in light of Jeremiah 31:16, 17 given in prayer. Their children had been liberated and were already safe in Canada.

"I was completely overcome," Edith recalled. "My children not only came from the land of the enemy, they came to their own border as the verse in Jeremiah had promised." The Bells were on the next train to Ontario. "We stepped down and were almost knocked over by our three children. It was joy unspeakable and full of glory. God's 'I wills' had not failed and we knew they never would."

In prayer, God whispers to us His secrets—things we would have no other way of knowing about except from the disclosure of His Holy Spirit.[1]

Wow!

---

[1] Robert J. Morgan, *More Real Stories for the Soul* (Nashville: Thomas Nelson, 2000) 71-73.

order

7

WHEN GOD WHISPERS
HIS SECRETS

After the angels accomplished the first component of their mission, they awakened vision in both Abraham and Sarah and united them in their purpose. The barrenness was soon to be broken. Within the year, a child would come at the time of spring—the season of Passover with new beginnings and new life. When the lambs are dropping and the hills turn green, a new sound would be heard in the tent of Abraham and Sarah—the cry of a newborn. This is the triumph of the spiritual over the natural. The couple that had passed the life-giving stage would give life. The ones who had been counted out, God would count in. Dismissed by nature, they had been appointed by God. Abraham's life changed as these angelic characters from the world beyond stepped into time and space to impart a transforming word. The barrenness was broken; laughter was born!

Now, for the first time a specific time frame had been placed on the promise (Genesis 18:10). Some translations say "in due season" (vv. 10, 14), but the Hebrew actually reads "at the time of reviving," or "at the time of life" (Hebrew, *ka'at chayah*). Literally, this means "in the spring." That places the birth within the timespan of a single year (later we learn that Abraham was 100 years old when the child was born; cf. 17:1).

Hearing God's Whispers

Turning to leave, the angels hesitated. Conferring among themselves, they mused, "Shall I not reveal to Abraham what we are about to do?" (see 18:17).

A third of the Bible is prophetic.[1] God doesn't travel through time like we do. He comes to us from our tomorrows, stepping out of our future into the present. He calls us into His plans and purposes. He is forever telling His children about a bright future He has for them. After the angels had awakened vision and capacity in Sarah, they now stirred Abraham. It was to be a part of the DNA of Abraham's descendants. Abraham would give birth to a nation—a nation meant to be intercessors.

The third movement in the chapter is that in entertaining God, He discloses His secrets. Here are the whisperings of God. Here is insight and knowl-

---

[1] Chip Ingram, *God—As He Longs for You to See Him* (Grand Rapids: Baker, 2004) 88.

edge gained supernaturally. C.S. Lewis observed, "It is in the process of being worshiped that God communicates His presence to man."[2] To His admirers, He discloses His treasures.

Wesley Duewel was traveling from India and fighting a fever. He prayed that he could locate one Christian to pray for him. He recalled the experience: "Suddenly I felt as if a human hand with a cool wet washcloth had wiped my brow. Instantly, my fever, headache, nausea, and sore throat were gone and I felt completely well. I thought, *Who prayed for me?*" Halfway around the world, the Holy Spirit had whispered the name of Wesley Duewel to an intercessor. They reported a heavy burden of prayer at the exact time of that day.[3]

The Call to Stand Between

God not only whispers His secrets to His intercessors, but as a loving and relational God, He also wakes His people up to pray for persons and things about which He cares. In prayer, you enter into partnership with the One whom God raised from the dead. And in prayer, we tap into that resurrection power. He has "raised us up with Christ and seated us with him in the heavenly realms" (Ephesians 2:6,

---

[2] C.S. Lewis, *Reflections on the Psalms* (New York: Harcourt, Brace, Jovanovich, 1958) 93.

[3] Wesley Duewel, *Touch the World Through Prayer* (Grand Rapids: Zondervan, 1986) 61-2.

That's what you told me we could do from the "good news center."

NIV). In prayer, we sit with Christ on His throne. In prayer, we reign with Christ and extend His rule in the earth. "You have no greater ministry or no leadership more influential than intercession . . . you reign as you prevail in prayer."[4]

D.L. Moody was a victim of the great Chicago fire in 1872. His church was destroyed and he went to England for study and reflection. He was soon discovered and prevailed upon to preach. He remembers greeting a cool and indifferent London congregation. He said later it was the most difficult preaching experience of his life. He became disheartened to think he had to face that congregation again that evening.

Arriving that night, he found a different atmosphere. The Holy Spirit was present in an evident way. He describes the experience, saying, "The power of an unseen world seemed to have fallen upon us!" He preached with persuasive power and invited those who wanted to become Christians to stand. Immedi-ately, 500 people stood to their feet. He thought the audience had misunderstood him. He repeated the invitation. Again, 500 people rose. He again asked them to take their seats and those who wanted Christ to step into the inquiry room. The whole crowd rushed to the room. Extra chairs were acquired. Moody, still disbelieving, asked only those who desired Christ to stand. Everyone stood. The pastor asked him to return the next evening.

What a story

---

[4] Duewel, 22.

That night, the crowd was larger. The meeting continued for 10 nights.

Moody was puzzled over the change. The frigid Sunday morning crowd had turned into a sizzling Sunday night audience. Subsequent evening encounters were decidedly marked by God's presence. *Why?* Moody wondered. He would soon learn that the sister of an invalid intercessor was present on that Sunday morning. She returned home to share with her invalid sister, Marianne Adelard, that Moody had preached that very morning in their church. Marianne had been praying for revival in the church she could no longer attend. She had heard of Moody. She kept an article about the evangelist under her pillow and had been praying that God would bring him to the city and to her church.

When she learned that he would return that evening and preach again, she dedicated the afternoon to interceding for him. She asked her sister to lock the door to her room and send her no dinner. She refused all fellowship in the afternoon. She prayed into the night. God obviously answered her prayers. In the birthday book signed by her visitors, you can find the name D.L. Moody. He not only visited her, but he was so convinced her prayers had won the victory that Moody engaged Marianne to pray for him until the day of her death. And she did.[5]

Samuel Chadwick would say, "It would seem as

[5] Bill Thrasher, *A Journey to Victorious Praying* (Chicago: Moody, 2003) 141-3.

if the biggest thing in God's universe is a man who prays!" Only one thing is more amazing in view of the power available through prayer—and that is a man who does not pray![6] Arthur Mathews says, "The spiritual history of a mission or a church is written in its prayer life."[7] *read on Wed night*

Prayer—the Highest Calling

Before Jesus called the Twelve to be with Him, He spent the night in prayer as preparation for that work (Luke 6:12, 13). When He had finished feeding the 5,000, He again hid away to spend time with His Father (Matthew 14:22, 23). After the busiest day of His recorded ministry, He did not opt to sleep in. He retreated for prayer (Mark 1:35). When He seemed overwhelmed by the sea of needy people around Him, sheep without a shepherd, He exhorted His disciples that the answer was not in more fevered activity, but in more prayer! Amazing. "Pray the Lord of the harvest to send out laborers" (see Matthew 9:35-38). He began His ministry in prayer. He ended His ministry in the Garden, in prayer. He prayed from the cross. And His final earthly act was to send His disciples to a prayer meeting in the Upper Room. Where was He going? To a prayer meeting in heaven,

---

[6] Samuel Chadwick, *The Path of Prayer* (Kansas City: Beacon Hill, 1931) 11-2.

[7] R. Arthur Mathews, *Born for Battle* (New York: Overseas Missionary Fellowship and Send the Light Trust, 1978) 74.

to pray the Father to send the Comforter. What is He doing now? He is ever interceding.

To move prayer to the periphery of a life, a family or church—even a city or a nation—is to move God to the forsaken edge as well. We have seen that demonstrated in our own culture. To allow prayer— no, to celebrate it—is to celebrate a caring and loving God, and to invite Him to know us and manifest Himself in our midst. O. Hallesby said, "A child of God can grieve Jesus in no worse way than to neglect prayer. . . . Many neglect prayer to such an extent that their spiritual life gradually dies out.[8]

Prayer is first and foremost an expression of an intimate relationship with God. Prayer includes discipline, but it is not merely a discipline. It involves setting aside a regular time and place, but it is not merely an item on our schedule. It includes asking for things we need, but it is not merely a shopping list of requests and rejoicings. It involves speaking to God and God speaking to us, but it is not merely an exchange of memoranda.

Prayer as Relationship

More than anything else, prayer is a relationship. When we reduce it to a regimen, we deprive ourselves of what all who knew God throughout the Scriptures expressed in their prayers: that God is alive, and that He knows us and lets Himself be known by us, that we can enjoy a deep and intimate

---

[8] O. Hallesby, *Prayer* (Minneapolis: Augsburg, 1936) 48-9.

personal relationship with Him in prayer.[9] Rosalind Rinker reminds us, "It isn't the words we say...it is the open-heart attitude which God looks for...the more natural the prayers, the more real He becomes."[10] We tend to view prayer as a process of gathering information about God and practicing certain techniques. But prayer is interpersonal communication; it matters far, far less how, when and what you say than how well you know Him to whom you pray.[11]

The son of a slave, William Seymour came to Texas to study the Bible, but Jim Crow laws prevented him from sitting in a classroom with a white instructor and white students. He would not be offended. He asked for the right to sit outside and listen. Charles Parham, the instructor, would declare prophetically that a new day was coming in which God would pour out His Spirit upon all flesh! Seymour's heart leaped within him. He longed to be a part of such an outpouring. But the very nature of his exclusion was a violation of one of the key principles in the coming eschatological flood of the Spirit into the soul of the church. It was as if God saw the line drawn between black and white, and He stepped over the line to join the banished Seymour. If anyone in that era might have been a candidate to serve as the leader of a new Pentecost, it would have been Parham.

[9] John Munro, "Prayer to a Sovereign God," *Interest*, Feb. 1990: 20. Quoted by Paul Cedar, *A Life of Prayer* (Nashville: Word, 1998) 40.
[10] Cedar, 41.
[11] Cedar, 42.

The Bible College was doing Seymour a great service by letting him even sit outside the classroom. They were, in light of the cultural divide between blacks and whites, extending an overdose of grace. God did not see it that way. Parham would end up playing a relatively minor role in a global spiritual explosion. Seymour, steeped in humility, would become the central figure in an outpouring of the Spirit that would invade Los Angeles and the world. Ripe with Aryanism, Los Angeles was about to be used as a showcase by God for a multicultural, class-and-kind diverse lovefest by Christians. And from the humble building on Azusa Street would burst forth the modern Pentecostal renewal.

J.I. Packer makes this observation:

> God's wisdom is not, and never was, pledged to keep a fallen world happy, or to make ungodliness comfortable. Not even to Christians has He promised a trouble-free life; rather the reverse. He has other ends in view for life in this world than simply to make it easy for everyone.
>
> What is He after? What is His goal? What does He aim at? . . . He plans that a great host of humankind should come to love and honor Him. His ultimate objective is to bring them to a state in which He is all in all to them, and He and they rejoice continually in the knowledge of each other's love—people rejoicing in the saving love of God, set upon them for all eternity, and God rejoicing in the responsive love

of people, drawn out of them by grace through the gospel.[12]

We "don't get it—understanding; without having Him—relationship!"[13] Paul declares that we have received "the Spirit who is from God, that we may understand what God has freely given us....The man without the Spirit does not accept the things that come from the Spirit of God, for they are foolishness to him, and he cannot understand them, because they are spiritually discerned" (1 Corinthians 2:12, 14, *NIV*).

The Power of His Presence

The church in Korea is growing four times faster than the population. Observers credit the surge of growth under the shadow of communism to the North to the open doors of Korean churches every morning at 5:00 for prayer. Many of these Korean Christians pray through the night on Fridays or spend whole weekends at prayer retreat centers. Korean pastors spend 90 minutes to three hours per day in prayer.[14]

Alvin J. Vander Griend tells about a church that started a 24-hour prayer effort, and as a part of their ministry, they began to pray for policemen of their small city. Within two months, without direct contact, two policemen began to attend the church and were

---

[12] J.I. Packer, *Knowing God* (Downers Grove, IL: Intervarsity, 1993) 91-2. Quoted by Ingram, 145.

[13] Ingram, 47.

[14] Alvin J. Vander Griend, *The Praying Church Sourcebook* (Grand Rapids: Church Development Resources, 1990, 1997) 13.

baptized. Six months later, with persistent prayer, the crime rate of the city had dropped from an average of 12 violent crimes in a six-month period to only two such crimes.[15]

The First Christian Church in Pampa, Texas, was struggling like a lot of other churches in North America. The struggle was not with worship, stewardship or anything identifiable. But all was not OK. There was a sense of stagnation. Enthusiasm was dwindling. The problem could only be addressed by prayer. The pastor called the church back to the basics. He wrote to them affirming his belief in the power of prayer. He began to teach and preach on prayer. He asked for a written commitment on the part of his members to join him in a yearlong pledge to pray like never before. About 100 people joined the "Prayer Power People" group. He started four classes on intercessory prayer. He set up a prayer chain. He established a telephone care line that provided updates on requests and other prayer concerns. He asked the Prayer Power People to meet 15 minutes before church school began each Sunday and pray, focusing on the pastor, the service, visitors and teachers. Everything began to change. Attitudes moved into the positive range. New music groups formed. Spontaneously, youth and young-adult groups formed for mission. The number of new members quadrupled in one year.[16]

[15] Vander Griend, 111.
[16] Vander Griend, 122.

Abraham entertained God, but he did not become familiar with God in a casual way! Jeremiah knew the same principle: "'Should you not fear me?' declares the Lord. 'Should you not tremble in my presence?'" (5:22, *NIV*). Abraham recognized that he was engaging the Sovereign: "I who am but dust and ashes have taken it upon myself to speak to the Lord" (Genesis 18:27). One translation says, *"ventured* to speak to the Lord" (*NASB*), or *"boldly dared* to speak." Humility and conviction are a powerful combination.

Paul Cedar lamented the condition of the American church: "I have had the privilege of visiting and ministering in hundreds of churches throughout the United States and in the world. One of my deepest concerns is how relatively few churches seem to experience the presence of Jesus Christ. Many local churches have become merely human organizations. They are frequently led by gifted pastors who seem to do little in the power of the Holy Spirit. Frequently when I am in that kind of environment, I am prompted by the Holy Spirit to ask the disturbing question, 'How long has it been since you have sensed the presence of Jesus Christ in this church?' Or, 'What would happen if Jesus showed up in your worship service next Sunday?'"[17] C.S. Lewis observed, "It is since Christians have largely ceased to think of the other world that they have become so ineffective in this one."[18]

Jeremiah 33:3 says, "Call to Me, and I will answer

---

[17] Cedar, 44.

[18] Quoted by Vernon McLellan, *Thoughts That Shaped the Church* (Wheaton: Tyndale, 2000) 256.

you, and show you great and mighty things, which you do not know." The phrase *mighty things* actually means "things that are hidden, inaccessible, things that are fenced in." Prayer penetrates barriers. It pierces hearts. It operates from the inside out. It knows no off-limits. The king's heart is in the hand of the Lord, and prayer massages it! Prayer knows no limited jurisdiction.[19]

Someone has said, "Prayer can do anything God can do!" That is not exactly true. The power of prayer is its access to the limitless power of God. Prayer has no power in itself. God has power, and He chooses to exercise it through the mystery of prayer. He is sovereign. He is a God who acts, but He chooses to act through prayer. Ronald Dunn notes, "Jesus rarely took the initiative in those miracles (recorded in the Gospels). Ordinarily, Jesus did not heal people until they asked Him to. Sometimes they almost had to chase Him down. Bartimaeus cried so long and so loud before Jesus stopped to listen that the crowd told that blind beggar to shut up (Mark 10:46-52)." It was the same with the Syrophoenician woman (Matthew 15:21-28). Jairus came to Jesus on behalf of his daughter (Mark 5:22-24, 35-43). The woman with the issue of blood pursued Him in the street (vv. 25-34). He declares, "Whatever you ask in My name, that I will do, that the Father may be glorified in the Son" (John 14:13).[20]

[19] Ronald Dunn, *Don't Just Stand There, Pray Something: The Incredible Power of Intercessory Prayer* (Nashville: Thomas Nelson, 1992) 42.

[20] Dunn, 52.

Abraham, foregoing the afternoon nap, fasting sleep, he sat at the threshold of his own tent. The watch—whether it is in the darkness of the night or the slumber hour of the Mideast afternoon—is not usually filled with excitement. It is that once-in-a-while occurrence that makes watching so strategically valuable. Is it possible that we miss certain things as a church because the watchers were not "on the wall" to receive the revelation? In ancient times, it was so important to have dutiful watchmen looking out for the city. The residents depended on the vigilance of those who served the lonely night hours. Today, we do not even understand the concept. It is hard for us to translate the idea into a need for 24-hour prayer over a city.

Dr. Bob Pierce was the founder of World Vision International. He was fond of using the term *God room*. Prayer was the means by which Dr. Pierce created "God room"—the time and place, the space and special means in which God used to do the impossible.

"God room" is always necessary when He calls you to a task bigger and grander than yourself. You say yes to the challenge, by faith. You determine to trust God and hang on for the ride. But you must do something else; you must pray. You gather your staff and supporters, your prayer partners—and you pray. You create "God room"! And then you watch God work. "Before you know it, the need is met. At the same time, you understand you didn't do it. God did it. You allowed Him room to work."[21]

The difference between Biblical faith and religion, between Christianity and witchcraft, is at some places so slight that great discernment is required to distin guish between the two. And yet, the test is so simple, even a child can understand it. And what is that test? Contentment comes with trusting God. A malcontent spirit attempts to control and illicit a particular outcome. Once you move from trusting God to trusting some means, some formula, some fetish, some ritual—you are moving onto the ground of spirit-manipulation.

This is an attempt to be the Sovereign ourselves. It goes all the way back to the Garden: "You shall be as gods!" Trust is a necessary requirement for a healthy relationship with God. When someone offers you the chance to see your future, to manipulate your future, recognize their offer for the idolatry it represents and for the doorway to certain evil to which it leads.

P.T. Forsyth declared, "Prayer is the atmosphere of revelation, in the strict and central sense of that word. It is the climate in which God's manifestation bursts open into inspiration."[22]

In his book *A Life of Prayer*, Paul Cedar tells about

21 Franklin Graham, *Rebel With a Cause* (Nashville: Nelson, 1995) 139.

22 P.T. Forsyth, *The Soul of Prayer* (Vancouver, B.C.: Regent, 1997, 2002) 32.

a young pastor who spoke to a group of ministers in a packed conference hall. He reported, "I would like to tell you why I believe in prayer."

He had graduated from seminary and had taken the assignment to pastor a small rural church that had developed a reputation for being rough on its pastors. Two previous pastors had not only left the congregation, they had also left the ministry—wounded. The pastor shared that the first months had gone fairly well. Then criticism of his preaching and complaints about his wife began. Then he could do nothing right. The situation worsened, and he felt that he was about to experience the same fate as the two pastors before him. He cried out to God and received a surprising response from God. He clearly sensed God instructing him to ask the most critical elders to pray with him. He resisted the idea, but it persisted. He recalled, "In fear and trembling, I approached the elders. . . . I asked them to pray with me." The elders agreed. They began to meet every Tuesday morning. Almost immediately, the change came—first, to their hearts. Then answers began to emerge. Visitors started to show up. Church attendance doubled. The pastor was now weeping as he told the story: "I have come to believe in the power of prayer. There is no other way to explain what has happened in our little church."[23]

---

[23] Cedar, 1-2.

MOVEMENT FOUR

Entertaining God and Commanding Generations

Genesis 18:19

"For I have known him, in order that he may command his children and his household after him, that they keep the way of the Lord, to do righteousness and justice, that the Lord may bring to Abraham what He has spoken to him."

One Man's Prayers and Four Generations

George McCluskey is not a famous name. But his story offers an inspiring example. He decided early in the life of his family to make an investment—one hour a day in prayer. He wanted his kids to follow Christ and establish homes that would honor the Lord. He prayed daily for his kids, his potential grandchildren and their children. His daily appointment with God in behalf of his children and the children after them was in the pre noon hour. And what was the result of such persistent praying?

His two daughters married men who entered the full-time ministry. From those godly couples came five grandchildren—four girls and one boy. All the girls married ministers. The grandson became a pastor. Then the first two great-grandchildren came along. George's prayers were still working. The two oldest boys of that generation went to the same college and were roommates. In the second year, one of them made the decision to enter the ministry. The other resisted. He broke the pattern, becoming the "black sheep" of the family, coloring outside the box. The first in four generations to resist entry into the ministry, he chose to study psychology. He graduated, earned a master's degree and then collected a doctorate.

He wrote a book that became a best-seller. Then another and yet another best-seller. He became a radio personality, giving Bible-based parenting advice to the nation. What is the name of this "black sheep" with a national radio program on more than 1,000 stations daily? It is James Dobson, the founder of Focus on the Family. He was George McCluskey's great-grandson, the product of his great-grandfather's prayers.[1]

The generational power of prayer is further illustrated in Dr. James Dobson's father, a devout praying man as well. In 1977, meeting God early in prayer, God gave him an assurance that his ministry would touch millions of people. He did not live to see it. He died of a heart attack the very next day. Before he died, he told his son that the God-given vision would be fulfilled through him. James Dobson's ministry was just beginning. How could he have known? In prayer, God whispers His secrets.

[1] Bill Thrasher, *A Journey to Victorious Praying* (Chicago: Moody, 2003) 122.

8

GENERATIONAL GENOCIDE

In a railway station in Austria, two men just happened to bump into one another. One of them was an alcoholic who begged the other for enough money to buy one more bottle of wine. The other stood back in simultaneous sadness and surprise that such an intelligent-looking man could sink to a life that consisted only of getting from one bottle to the next. The alcoholic explained his delinquency on a life of bad luck. The cards of life had been stacked against him. His mother died when he was young. His father had beaten him, as well as his brothers and sisters, mercilessly. Then, World War I had come along and permanently separated the family. "I never had a chance," he reasoned. "This is strange," his new acquaintance responded. "My background is similar to yours. I, too, lost my mother when I was young.

My father was also brutal, and the war separated
me from my family as well. I felt that I had no choice
but to try to overcome the circumstances rather than
to be overcome by them." The two men continued
to talk, comparing notes. They made an impossible
discovery. They were brothers—blood brothers. Out
of the same family, launched with almost identical
handicaps and hopes, one had succeeded; the other
had succumbed. It was not life that had been the
factor, not the hard knocks or difficult challenges.
It was the choices each of them had made.[1] Lot and
Abraham came from the same stock, but ended up
in different worlds.

Abraham had a brother named Haran, the father
of Lot. He died an untimely death. Abraham's father,
Terah, appears to have never recovered. The whole
party—Terah, Abram and Lot—were all leaving Ur of
the Chaldeans, headed for Canaan. Had Terah heard
from Yahweh? Was he being led by God? When the
party reached a city that bore the name of his beloved
son, Haran, he could go no farther. Terah died there.
And so did his dream of Canaan. Abram would
adopt Lot. He would love him like a son. The feeling
would never be mutual. Abram was on a divinely
inspired journey. Lot saw "dollars." If Terah had not
been so overwhelmed by his loss, would we speak
of Terah today and not Abraham? Not everyone God
calls lives up to his or her calling! If we could only

[1] Brian L. Harbour, *Famous Couples of the Bible* (Nashville:
Broadman, 1979) 99-100.

understand there is more at stake than us and this present moment. Listen to the Angel of the Lord: "Have I not known him in order that he would command his family after Me?" (see Genesis 18:19). He saw in Abraham a thousand generations. In Abraham, history pivots. In this moment, destiny and blessing was procured for his children's children's children.

Living in Vegas

Traveling the King's Highway, you would have seen the exit sign to Sodom and Gomorrah. The cluster of five cities was located on the southeast side of the Dead Sea, just a few miles off that ancient trade route. Sodom was a community built on a radical order. Some have said it was the Las Vegas of the ancient world. The contrast between Genesis 18 and 19 is striking. The two chapters are only understood when treated together.

In Genesis 18, a new nation is to be launched in the spring. In Genesis 19, a decaying culture is destroyed. Abraham and Lot would be forever separated after this moment. Their choices had sent them and their generational offspring in different directions.

Lot had seen the fertile area cradling the cities of the plain. He had immediately concluded that was the spot for him. He first moved near Sodom. Then, he moved into Sodom. It happened so subtly. The first few trips to the general store in Sodom must have been eye-popping experiences. Then the shock

137

wore off. *There would be advantages to living here. It would cut down on the mileage on the camels. It isn't as bad as it appears from the outside. You have to know whom to trust. You learn the safe streets.* The rationalizations flowed.

Unlike the barrenness that now surrounds the Dead Sea, the area around ancient Sodom was "well watered everywhere...like the garden of the Lord" (13:10). There probably was no place like it anywhere in the region. It was New Orleans, Amsterdam and Palm Springs all rolled into one, a hedonistic heaven. Find a seat near the swimming pool...have a drink ...listen to a song. It was a city filled with buffets—eat all you want...relax, take it easy. Everyone was living the "good life"! No panhandlers were allowed on the street. The needy were kept neatly out of sight, and there was nothing to distract anyone from a full baptism in pleasure. Ezekiel would say of her (Sodom):

> She and her daughter had pride, fullness of food, and abundance of idleness; neither did she strengthen the hand of the poor and needy. And they were haughty and committed abomination before Me; therefore I took them away as I saw fit (16:49, 50).

Peter would use stronger language, charging that Sodom was guilty of filthy conduct, a wicked city that tormented the righteous and was characterized by lawless deeds (2 Peter 2:6-8). These were not simply sinners; they were blatant sinners. Mardi Gras comes on the cusp of Lent. It is an "in-your-face" celebration of

138

immorality in the days before Easter—when Christians remember that their sin cost Christ His life. Such irreverence is breathless. Such disrespect for the Cross is unfathomable. Sodom was a Mardi-Gras kind of city.

Sodom and Gomorrah have become code words symbols of cities that champion hedonism, flaunt morality, have party spots, and lawless places with an anything-goes-here attitude. Its people were morally sadistic, relationally irresponsible, reckless with fragile lives, people users, pleasure-crazy.

Intercessors and Angels

While the angels prepared to enter Sodom, the Angel of the Lord had Abraham on the hill overlooking the cities of the plain. Lot spotted the strangers in the city square, not recognizing them as angels. Knowing the nighttime appetites and habits of the city, that men would prowl through the streets looking for sexual action, he knew they would be victims if left in the street. He pleaded with them to take shelter in his home. He provided hospitality, but the word was soon out on the street that he was housing visitors. When his doorbell rang, the men of the city wanted to meet these guests.

When the Earth Mourns

It was the "cry of Sodom" that alerted God (Genesis 18:20, 21). The word *cry* (*zaaq*) means "to shriek from anguish or danger." Did Lot cry out? That is doubtful because he had to be practically dragged from the

139

city. It was the intercession of Abraham that saved Lot. Did Abraham cry out? No, the Angel of the Lord came by to wake up prayer in him. Did Sodom cry out? No objection came from the city fathers.[2]

Was it Sodom's victims of human violence and lust? Was it the earth that cried out? Was it creation groaning? Now that sin is multiplied and out of control, does nature and created order have some kind of moral alarm system more sensitive than that of sinful man? Does nature still observe limits that we dare to transgress? Does the earth shiver with anticipation of the coming Judgment?

Thomas Merton says, "There has never been a bomb invented that is half so powerful as one mortal sin—and yet there is no positive power in sin, only negation, only annihilation."[3] Does nature itself rise up and punish us at times when we have transgressed limits that even she knows are wicked? Dostoyevsky reminds us in *The Brothers Karamazov*, "If God does not exist—everything is permissible."[4] For Sodom, God did not exist, at least not a God who would object to hedonism. And everything was permissible.

Why Was Sodom Destroyed?

Sodom was a community built on a radical social and religious order. Its families did not conform to

---

[2] Joseph Mattera, *Ruling in the Gates* (Lake Mary, FL: Creation House, 2003) 59.

[3] Quoted by Vernon McLellan, *Thoughts That Shaped the Church* (Wheaton: Tyndale, 2000) 224.

[4] Quoted by McLellan, 56.

the norm of God's plan in Genesis—a man and a woman in satisfying union. Here a different arrangement existed. For 25 years, God waited patiently for an alignment of unity and faith in Sarah and Abraham. From this man-woman union, God wanted to bring forth a new nation of ordered and healthy families. As the new model family gave birth to a nation, a cluster of city-states with disordered families would perish.

This destruction was not due to their sexual behavior, it was tied to the rejection of those God sent. They did not receive strangers with grace. They did not know how to entertain those whom God sent. Here is the contrast: Receiving God and those He sends breaks barrenness, opens the womb of promise, causes us to be called friends of God, qualifies us for divine disclosures—and more. Rejecting those whom God sends is the opposite. The result is always judgment. Jesus would emphasize this in Luke 10 when He sent out the 70. They were to look for a man of peace, enter the house and speak peace over it (vv. 5, 6). If the city received those God sent, God's kingdom power would be evidenced in that city. If the city rejected those sent, the judgment would be greater than that on Sodom (v. 12). Receiving those sent by God results in the embrace of God himself. Jesus said to the Jewish establishment, "Your house is left to you desolate . . . you shall see Me no more till you say, 'Blessed is He who comes in the name of the Lord!'" (Matthew 23:38, 39).

In the desolation of the cities of the plain, we see a picture of the coming worldwide Judgment. That judgment is not due to sin that can be forgiven. It is due to the rejection of the One sent from God—Jesus, His Son.

Passover

The date of this night on Israel's calendar would later take on greater significance. This was the night the Death Angel would pass through Egypt hundreds of years later and rescue Abraham's seed from slavery. This was the night of Passover.[5] But there would be no Passover in Sodom. There might have been. Abraham was pleading for one, but there needed to be seeds of righteousness in the city for potential change to be there. In Sodom, there was no repentance, no promise of change. The result? Judgment!

It had been on a Passover night that Abraham had entered into a crossover covenant with God when he received the promise of new possessions in Canaan (Genesis 15:1-21). It was at the Passover that both the exodus from Egypt and the entrance into the threshold of the new Promised Land occurred (Joshua 5:10).[6] And it was in that season that Jericho would be destroyed, with the exception of Rahab, who would be saved by displaying the scarlet thread, a reflection of the blood on the doorposts in Egypt. The protection of Israel against the Midianites (Judges 7:1-25), the

---

[5] H. Clay Trumbull, *The Threshold Covenant* (Kirkwood, MO: Impact Christian Books, 2000) 192.

[6] Trumbull, 192.

Assyrians (2 Kings 19:20-36; 2 Chronicles 32:1-22), the Medes and the Persians (Esther 9:12-19), and the overthrow of Babylon (Daniel 5:1-30) were all at the Passover season.[7]

The Passover night is that time when Yahweh takes Himself a bride. When Hebrews shut themselves away into their homes on Passover night, it is not merely from the world and its plagues. It is to Yahweh that they commit themselves. They cross the blood-stained threshold. And in the breaking of bread and the drinking of the wine, they enter a family covenant with their saving God. Here is the ultimate source of the idea that a bride is carried across the threshold on the wedding night. On this night, God becomes the husband of Israel. And from this night forth, any unfaithfulness on her part will be called adultery or fornication. Her lovers will incur the wrath of a jealous Husband. He is married to her. She resides under the protection of His sacred threshold. Jeremiah looks forward to the restoration of the marriage while he looks back at the sacred beginning:

> I have loved you with an everlasting love ... with lovingkindness I have drawn you.... I will build you ... O virgin of Israel! You shall again be adorned with your tambourines, and go forth in the dances of those who rejoice.
>
> They shall come and sing ... streaming to the goodness of the Lord ... they shall sorrow no more.... I will turn their mourning to joy, will comfort them, and make them rejoice rather than sorrow.

7 Trumbull, 193.

> Behold, the days are coming, says the Lord,
> when I will make a new covenant with the
> house of Israel and with the house of Judah—
> not according to the covenant that I made with
> their fathers in the day that I took them by the
> hand to lead them out of the land of Egypt,
> My covenant which they broke, though I was
> a husband to them, says the Lord. But this is
> the covenant that I will make with the house
> of Israel . . . I will put My law in their minds,
> and write it on their hearts; and I will be their
> God, and they shall be My people. No more
> shall every man teach his neighbor, and every
> man his brother, saying, "Know the Lord,"
> for they all shall know Me, from the least of
> them to the greatest of them. . . . I will forgive
> their iniquity, and their sin I will remember no
> more (31:3, 4, 12, 13, 31-34).

This Passover brings death to the cities of the plain.
The next Passover will bring life into Abraham and
Sarah's tent. Isaac (Laughter) will be born. Passover
is a night for choices. It is no longer a fixed date on
the calendar. Passover is every night. It is the time
God calls men and women to make a decision—to
leave Sodom and Gomorrah, to flee Egypt.

Ultimately a Passover will come to the entire earth.
On that night, God will call from the earth those who
would stand with Him and flee the world. Intercessors
will be praying. Angels will be dispatched and actively
protecting. The Spirit will be convicting and drawing.
But every man will have to will, by grace, his separa-
tion from this world to the one to come.

144

Sodom will die. Gomorrah will perish. And this world will pass away. Abraham's seed will become the focus of God's love. The city-states perish due to their self-centered foundation. The new nation will blossom due to the servant heart of its head Abraham. God will call them to serve His purposes in the earth as faithfully as their father Abraham. In time they will fail God, but He will never fail them.

Allowing Sodom Into Our Souls

Sodom was not a safe city. In its streets, strangers were not protected. Righteousness and justice were swept aside. Personal sexual appetites overwhelmed the concern for the protection and rights of others. The whole culture of the city was skewed toward personal pleasure, even at the expense of others. The sexual perversion was only the fruit of sick and self-centered hearts. Lot was not comfortable with the sexual atmosphere of the city, yet it might have been his own bent toward greed that made him feel at home in the city to begin with.

How do we end up in compromises? How could any believer choose to make a home in Sodom — unless he was there as a missionary? Tragically, Lot was not a missionary. He sat in the gates (Genesis 19:1), indicating that he was clearly a citizen-leader of Sodom! Was he an elder of the city? How had he gained that level of respect? Abraham loved Lot. When the king of Babylon and his allies had raided Sodom and taken Lot hostage, Abraham had turned his servants into soldiers and had routed the kings, liberating Lot as well as Sodom and Gomorrah (see ch. 14). That victory may have won Lot a spot on the city council. Now, his influence with them fails. "And they said, 'Stand back!...This one came in to stay here, and he keeps acting as a judge; now we will deal worse with you than with them.' So they pressed hard against the man Lot" (19:9). He must have tried at times to reprove the men of Sodom for their sin, acting as a conscience for the city. No more.[8]

Large compromises are not usually the way we backslide. We rarely leap out of fellowship with God and walk contrary to His values. Rather, we give in to little compromises of the heart—little rationalized actions. One step, then two. One little jump, then another. We may not even be aware of the drift that is taking place.

Two of Lot's daughters married men who found his plea to leave the city for their own protection laughable. He had not influenced them. He was unsuccessful in evangelizing his own family. He lost two of his daughters to the values of the city. He left without them. How different than the generational blessing Abraham had secured for his seed.

Angels Protecting and Abraham Praying

At Lot's door, the men of the city clamored like a mob. "Bring out the men!" In the middle of the mob

---

[8] Trumbull, 77.

146

scene, the angels pulled Lot back inside his own house, "and they struck the men who were at the doorway of the house with blindness, both small and great, so that they became weary trying to find the door" (v. 11). Miraculously, they were not so blind that they couldn't see. They simply couldn't see the door! They were utterly disoriented.

Dianne was a missionary kid. She lived in a missionary compound in Jordan. Her story is rich with God's intervening grace and fraught with mystery. Playing in the yard of the enclosed compound, she recalls the morning an angry mob marched down the street with murder in their eyes. It was a frightening moment. The gate opened and the mob was inside. Then suddenly, in what looked like a *Keystone Cops* comedy, the whole group turned abruptly left. With dazed looks in their eyes, as if they were seeing something the children could not see, they scrambled to the left wall of the compound and poured over it like fire ants. It would be weeks before the mystery was solved. Her grandmother in Chicago would write that she had been awakened in the night to pray for them. She had to pray. Consumed by a certain sense of peril, she fell to her knees and prayed until the burden lifted. The date and time of the prayer episode? Yes! The same date and time of the mob's march into the compound and their subsequent blind scurry over the wall.[9]

---

[9] Bill Thrasher, *A Journey to Victorious Praying* (Chicago: Moody, 2003) 50-1.

Next, the angels urged Lot, "Whomever you have in the city—take them out of this place! For we will destroy this place, because the outcry against them has grown great before the face of the Lord, and the Lord has sent us to destroy it" (vv. 12, 13).

Sodom had not entertained God's ambassadors very well. The result was judgment. When Jesus sent His disciples out, two by two, He told them to look in the village for a worthy home. Finding that home, they were to make it their ministry headquarters. They were to speak peace over it. And upon the city, they were to release a healing stream of God's grace. The city would be blessed and favored by God. Extraordinary things would occur. But if that city did not receive the men of peace, then Jesus warned it would be worse for them than it was for Sodom and Gomorrah (see Matthew 10:1-15).

The difference between blessing and curse is bound up in whether or not we receive the Lord and those He sends. "O Jerusalem, Jerusalem, the one who kills the prophets and stones those who are sent to her! How often I wanted to gather your children together, as a hen gathers her chicks under her wings, but you were not willing! See! Your house is left to you desolate; for I say to you, you shall see Me no more till you say, 'Blessed is He who comes in the name of the Lord!'" (23:37-39).

The angels practically dragged Lot out of the city: "Escape for your life! Do not look behind you nor stay anywhere in the plain. Escape to the mountains, lest you be destroyed" (Genesis 19:17). Stuart Briscoe says of Lot, he had "flirted with Sodom and found himself seduced."[10] He had held himself back from the active sin of Sodom, but he breathed the spirit of the city without the need of a respirator. Only an intercessor on a hill, pleading with God and activating the grace of God, had saved him. He probably never knew that! The hold on his wife cost their marriage and her life. The influence on his daughters led to drunkenness and incest.

Paul says with gentleness he must correct his opponents, "for God might grant them repentance that would lead them to a full knowledge of the truth, and they might recover their senses and escape from the devil's trap in which they have been caught by him to do his will" (see 2 Timothy 2:25, 26). Men have been "taken alive"—in warfare. They are blind and in bondage. Their only hope is grace for repentance.

Lot would flee the city with the shirt on his back. All his wealth would perish in the brimstone fire. Running for his life, he would leave two daughters in the hands of certain death. And he would see his wife turn back, shriek in terror, but he would not be able to pause and mourn for her. It was a sad day for a man who came close to having it all. That night he must have reflected on the years he had spent with his uncle, Abraham. They were good years,

---

[10] Stuart Briscoe and Lloyd J. Ogilvie, gen. ed., *The Communicator's Commentary—Genesis* (Waco: Word, 1987) 172.

prosperous and kind years, but he had wanted more. Abraham had been content with something deep inside. Lot had looked for external pleasures. No amount of "more!" could ever satisfy his lust. Now he had lost it all. He was depressed and confused, but the lowest point was yet to come. Stuart Briscoe sums it up like this:

> Eventually the old man succumbed to the scheming of his unscrupulous daughters, drank himself into a stupor, and engaged in incestuous relations which were to produce offspring from whom would come long chapters of even sadder history.[11]

Erwin W. Lutzer declares the following:

> Better to love God and die unknown than to love the world and be a hero; better to be content with poverty than to die a slave to wealth; better to have taken some risks and lost than to have done nothing and succeeded at it; better to have lost some battles than to have retreated from the war; better to have failed when serving God than to have succeeded when serving the devil. What a tragedy to climb the ladder of success only to discover that the ladder was leaning against the wrong wall![12]

---

[11] Briscoe, 173.
[12] Quoted by McLellan, 229.

9

SORTING THROUGH THE
ASHES OF SODOM

The cities were destroyed catastrophically. Towers collapsed and the bodies were left to decay where they died. The walls of both cities seemed to have imploded. Whatever happened to the cities happened suddenly, without warning, and with disastrous results. According to the Biblical record, only Lot and his two daughters escaped.

Why were Sodom and Gomorrah destroyed? Some scholars now believe that Sodom and Gomorrah engaged in a cultic worship pattern that combined sexual and religious activity, probably related to the fertility cult of the Canaanites. The city was sexually alive. And the sexual practices were homosexual in nature. But, as we noted earlier, Sodom and Gomorrah were not destroyed precisely because of sexual sin. The sexual aberrance of the city was only a symptom of the rejection of God and God's order. And the root of that rebellion was pride.

Isaiah warned Israel, "The look on their countenance witnesses against them, and they declare their sin as Sodom; they do not hide it. Woe to their soul!" (3:9). Peter gives Lot credit for being "tormented" living there (2 Peter 2:7, 8). He was not comfortable, but his kids had come to see the life of the city as normal. This was the danger Jesus warned about— "eating and drinking, marrying and giving in marriage" (Matthew 24:38). It was life like any other place, but it wasn't any other place. When Lot suggested to his sons-in-law that a special judgment was coming to the city, they took him as seriously as we take someone giving a report of his recent encounter with Martians. "Get up, get out of this place; for the Lord will destroy this city!" (Genesis 19:14). His wife resisted. His daughters did not want to leave. They had become comfortable with sordid Sodom.

When Cities Disappear

Excavations are now going on in the ancient cities of the plain. Two geologists suggest that a massive earthquake, more than 7.0 on the Richter scale, occurred in the upper end of the 4,000-mile-long Great Rift Valley. That fault line stretches from Mozambique on the east coast of Central Africa and reaches northwest to encompass the whole of the Red Sea, and then northward through the Jordan Valley into Syria.[1]

---

[1] Joseph Gardner, gen. ed., *Reader's Digest Atlas of the Bible* (Pleasantville, NY: The Reader's Digest Association, 1981) 39.

The Dead Sea area is full of bitumen (tar) pits, rich with deposits of petroleum and natural gas. All of these are combustible materials. Forced through the crust of the earth by a severe quake,[2] the earthquake would have ignited these "light fractions of hydro-carbons escaping from underground reservoirs," resulting in something like a rain of fire and brimstone. So severe was the disruption to nature that the flow into the Dead Sea from the Jordan was disrupted for days.[3] Bolts of lightning would have lit up the darkened sky, streaking from the billowing clouds of volcanic debris, fueled by sulphurous gases. It would have been an eerie site. The area once called "the Vale of Siddim" hosted the five cities. It can be located northwest of Al Karak and just south of the tongue of land jutting out from the Jordanian side of the Dead Sea. The seismic event caused the land to sink 50 feet, leaving the cities buried under the waters of the Dead Sea.[4]

The destruction was sudden and permanent. Buried in the southeast corner of the Dead Sea, sonar has detected trees standing, preserved, at a depth of 23 feet. On the eastern shore of the Dead Sea, additional ruins have been explored in association with the Arab city Babe dh-Dhra, thought to be the extended ruins of Sodom. The heavily fortified and settled city

---

[2] Randall Price, *The Stones Cry Out* (Eugene, OR: Harvest, 1997) 118.

[3] Price, 110.

[4] Robert Faid, *A Scientific Approach to Biblical Mysteries* (Green Forest, AR: New Leaf, 1993) 154, 155.

had walls as thick as 23 feet. There were extensive walled buildings, broad and wide open-air areas, houses, cemeteries with thousands buried there—evidence of a large population. Large collapsed monoliths average 13 feet in length. They present the possibility of a shrine for cultic rites. Evidence of a Canaanite temple has been found with its semi-circular altar along with numerous cultic objects. The town is covered by a thick ash layer. Posts of buildings are charred. Roofs reveal destruction by fire. Bricks are discolored as a result of intense heat.[5]

Archaeologist Bryant Wood explains:

> The evidence would suggest that this site of Babe dh-Dhra is the Biblical city of Sodom . . . what they discovered was that the fire did not begin inside the building but rather the fire started on the roof of the building, then the roof burned through, collapsed into the interior and then the fire spread inside the building. And this was the case in every single channel house they excavated.[6]

Another ancient city, Numeira, just south of Babe dh-Dhra, is identified with Gomorrah. It too was destroyed by extensive burning. Among the ruins was a large stash of barley seeds used in that day, not only to make bread, but also to manufacture beer. The food stores indicate cities of plenty, "fullness of bread" (Ezekiel 16:49, KJV).[7]

---

[5] Price, 113-5.

[6] Quoted by Price, 117.

[7] Price, 123.

Abraham and Lot: Two Kinds of Churches

Abraham looked for a city with foundations, whose builder and maker is God (Hebrews 11:10). He was a pilgrim here. He was a man of faith—a righteous man and a godly father. Never at home in this earth, his heart longed for God. Lot found his city and settled there. What a contrast.

There is one church like Abraham and another like Lot. One church looks toward Sodom and, despite its rich surroundings, plenteous food and water, it could never be at home in such a place. That church intercedes for Sodom. It weeps for its salvation. Then there is another church, one like Lot, that has moved into the world of Sodom. It is vexed by the unrighteousness of the place, but not enough to leave. It holds to higher righteous values than Sodom, but it is not enough of a righteous influence to change the city. It is losing its own kids to Sodom. The spirit of the city has overcome this church. It is too much at home in Sodom. This church sits in the gates of the city, still holding a position of power, but in practice, it has no influence over the city.

John says, "We know that we are of God, and the whole world lies under the sway of the wicked one" (1 John 5:19). The word *lies* is the picture of a mother cradling her baby in her arms and rocking it to sleep. So the Evil One cuddles our world, cradles it in his embrace. He is rocking this world into a deadly sleep.[8]

---

[8] Ronald Dunn, *Don't Just Stand There, Pray Something: The Incredible Power of Intercessory Prayer* (Nashville: Thomas Nelson, 1992) 120.

This sleepiness is like "a veil"! The "god of this age has blinded" the minds of those who do not believe the gospel (2 Corinthians 4:3, 4). "The natural man does not receive the things of the Spirit . . . they are foolishness to him." These things have to be "spiritually discerned" (1 Corinthians 2:14).

The day after the intense intercession of Genesis 18, "Abraham went early in the morning to the place where he had stood before the Lord" (19:27). From a distance of 30 miles,[9] he saw "the smoke of the land which went up like the smoke of a furnace" (v. 28).

If the destruction involved an earthquake, as some speculate, it had no doubt jarred him awake. With his heart in his throat, he had to know that tragedy had come to the party city. Lot would never recover from his compromises. Abraham would forever reap rewards for his persistence. Lot's daughters would bear the evidence of his immorality in the spring of the year. Sarah would bear the son of promise in the same season.

Heavenly Encounters and Human Destiny

Abraham is an extraordinary figure. Four millennia after his death, he seems to still live. The land he put under the soles of his feet is the most disputed piece of earth on the planet. From him, we trace three of the earth's faiths—Judaism, Christianity and Islam. Perhaps no other figure in all of history commands

[9] Faid, 152.

such an influential position apart from Christ himself. What if he had been too busy that afternoon to pray? Too sleepy to entertain these three strangers? What blessings do we miss because we do not entertain God?

He was a nomad whose only title deed was to a burial site. A shepherd, wealthy by bedouin standards, he hated conflict. He was a contented man with a spot of restless, unfinished destiny in his soul. What sets him apart? Why does God look after Abraham's children 4,000 years after his death? Is there something we could learn that might procure blessing for our children, even 10 generations hence?

The salvation of a city and the root of a godly nation is in ordered homes. Faith rises or falls on the back of the family. Western culture is utterly individualistic. And we are blind to how acculturated we are. We see the church as a collection of individuals. It is not. It is a collection of homes—homes which should be Biblically ordered. We divide, rather than unite the family. We divide them by age and gender. We place individual interest over corporate care and responsibility. Rather than unify the family, we dismantle it.

Healthy churches demand healthy homes. Ordered churches demand ordered homes. Church problems are home problems perpetrated on the church. And the disorder of our churches is the reflection of the disorder in our homes. Leaders for our churches are not to be drawn from the most successful, the most articulate, the wealthiest, and the most worldly-wise and connected. The Western church is drunk with celebrity, impressed by prestige and position. Not so in the New Testament. The leaders there were men whose homes were ordered. "For if a man does not know how to rule his own house, how will he take care of the church of God?" (1 Timothy 3:5).

The angelic visit impacts the home of Abraham and Sarah, and that changes the course of the nation. When Peter discusses a model for the home, he offers us the couple that entertained God—Abraham and Sarah (1 Peter 3:5-7). The absence of prayer in the home is more damaging than the absence of prayer at church. Dunn says of prayer for our children:

> We can wrap them in the arms of intercession and march them through the fires of hell and into the gates of heaven. This is the inheritance we can leave to our children—an inheritance of prayer, prayers lifted to God long before the children were born, prayers answered long after we are gone.[10]

✳ The Long Reach of Prayer *wow!*

You may not recognize the name W.P. MacKay, but you have probably sung his most famous hymn, "Revive Us Again." His mother was a godly woman who wanted him to embrace Christ. She would tell him about Jesus. He would find her engaged in passionate prayer for his soul, to no avail. The more

---

[10] Dunn, 20.

she wrestled with God for his salvation, the more he pulled in the opposite direction. He rose above his humble roots, qualifying for medical school. He pushed faith aside, attempting to drive God from his thoughts. His lifestyle was wicked, he was nearing infidelity as a worldview. Deep inside, he was haunted by the purity of his mother's love and her prayerful passion for his highest good.

In the hospital where he worked, a laborer was presented to him with serious injuries from a considerable fall. The case was hopeless. All that could be done was to comfort the man. He seemed to realize his terminal condition. Despite the injury, he was fully alert. Dr. MacKay recalls, "He asked about his condition. As it was in vain to keep the truth from him, I gave him my opinion in as cautious a manner as I could. 'Have you any relatives we can notify?'" He was alone in the world. His only wish was to see his landlady. He owed her a small amount of money, and he wanted her to bring him "the Book!" "What book?" Dr. MacKay questioned. "Oh, just ask her for the Book, she will know," was his reply. He lingered for a week, then died. Each day during that period, Dr. MacKay visited him at least once a day. "What struck me most was the quiet, almost happy expression that was constantly on his face. I knew he was a Christian." Still, Dr. MacKay could not bring himself to talk about such matters.

After his death, the nurse asked, "What shall we do with this?" holding up a book in her hand. "What kind of book is it?" asked MacKay. "It was the Bible of the poor man. His landlady brought it on her second visit. As long as he was able to read it, he did so, and when he was unable to do so anymore, he kept it under his bedcover."

Dr. MacKay took the Bible in hand. It had been a long time since he held a copy of the Book! Opening it, he could not believe his eyes. His name was written in the front of the Bible, in the handwriting of his own beloved mother. It was the Bible she had given him when he left home. In medical school, he had sold it for a small sum. Beneath his name was the verse his mother had chosen for him! He recalls, "I stood as if in a dream, but I regained my self-control, managing to conceal before those present my deep emotion. In seemingly indifferent manner and tone, I answered the nurse, 'The book is old and has hardly any value, let me keep it.'"

The Bible had been used frequently. The leaves were loose, some torn. The cover was worn. Every page gave evidence that it had been read often. Many verses were underscored. "I read some of the precious verses, and a word I had heard in the days of my youth came back to memory. With a deep sense of shame, I looked upon the Book, the precious Book. It has given comfort and refreshing to the unfortunate man in his last hours. It has been a guide to him in eternal life, so that he had been enabled to die in peace and happiness. And this Book, the last gift of my mother, I had actually sold for a ridiculous price."

The encounter would change forever the hard heart of the doctor. He came full circle, back to the faith of his childhood. A gift he had rejected had found him on the wings of his mother's prayers.[11] Prayer affects our children, even after we are gone.

Satan has no defense against this weapon; he does not have an anti-prayer missile. "The unbeliever has many defenses against our evangelistic efforts. He can refuse to attend church. If he does show up, he can shift into neutral and count the cracks in the ceiling. You can visit his home, but he doesn't have to let you in. Hand him a tract on the street, and he can throw it away. Get on TV, and he can switch channels. Call him on the phone, and he can hang up. But he cannot prevent the Lord Jesus from knocking at the door of his heart in response to our intercession. People we cannot reach any other way can be reached by way of the throne of grace."[12]

We don't pray because we have no other option; we pray because it is our first and best option—with no others comparable.

[11] Robert J. Morgan, *More Real Stories for the Soul* (Nashville: Thomas Nelson, 2000) 137-40.

[12] Dunn, 20.

10

THE SACRED
THRESHOLD

When the angels showed up, Abraham was sitting in the tent door. We miss the importance of that resting spot. He might have found it cooler under the shade of the nearby oak trees. His place is not incidental. The ancient door is a place of covenant. "The primitive altar of the family would seem to have been the threshold, or doorsill, or entranceway of the home dwelling place."[1]

F.B. Meyer, the great preacher, believed that "wherever Abraham pitched his tent, he built an altar. And long after the tent was shifted, the altar stood to show where the man of God had been."[2]

---

[1] H. Clay Trumbull, *The Threshold Covenant* (Kirkwood, MO: Impact Christian Books, 2000) 3.

[2] F.B. Meyer, *Abraham, God's Friend* (Westchester, IL: Good News, 1962) 14.

The doorway was a sacred place. In some societies, people coming or going kiss the door. Conservative Jews do it to this day. In pre-communist Russia, crosses often adorned the doorways of Christians. In Mexico among the Indians, an altar was near the door of every house.[3] The very presence of fire around an ancient homesite was not merely utilitarian. The fire was holy. It was sacred fire. It was altar fire. In ancient Greece, the mother of a freshly married daughter would be the fire carrier. Marching with her daughter to her bridal home, the mother of the bride would bear a flaming torch that had been lit with fire from the maternal household. She would light the fire in the new home. Similar customs were observed in Rome and India. Sacred fire was required for the newly created sacred home. The Mordvins in Russia would prepare a huge candle to light on the wedding day. Smaller candles were used at the church ceremony, but the larger candle would be placed in the doorway, at the threshold of the new couple's anticipated residence. The father of the bridegroom would light the candle and offer a prayer for the launch of the new family.[4]

In 1599, Elizabeth, the daughter of Henry II, was married to Philip II of Spain by the bishop of Paris. The ceremony was not performed in the church, but at the door of the cathedral of Notre Dame. In those days, vows were stated at the threshold, and then

---

[3] Trumbull, 17-9.
[4] Trumbull, 37-8.

mass was celebrated in the cathedral. As late as 1873, in Essex, England, the first part of a marriage ceremony was performed at the door of the church, the latter part in the sanctuary.[5]

On the night of the Exodus from Egypt, each family offered a sacrifice and the blood of that lamb was applied to the doorposts of the home. The Death Angel passed through the land. Nothing prevented him from entering a home through the wall or the ceiling. But the angel, instead, noted the door of each home. On finding the blood of the lamb at the doorway, the angel would not cross the threshold and enter that sacred space.

> And you shall take a bunch of hyssop, dip it in the blood that is in the basin, and strike the lintel and the two doorposts with the blood that is in the basin. And none of you shall go out of the door of his house until morning (Exodus 12:22).

Even today, it is considered unlucky to tread *on* the threshold. The word *pesah*, or *Passover*, may refer to the ancient practice of "leaping over" or passing over the threshold after it had been sanctified with the blood of the threshold covenant.[6]

To this day, modern Jews preserve the sacred idea of the threshold by obeying Deuteronomy 6:4-9 and 11:13-21: "You shall write them on the doorposts of your house and on your gates" (6:9; 11:20). At one

---

[5] Trumbull, 127.

[6] *http://www.jewishencyclopedia.com/view.jsp?artid=199&letter=T.*

time, these words may have been inscribed on the doorposts. Throughout the ancient Near East, inscriptions have been found by archaeologists on liminal spaces. Stone plaques outside Samaritan dwellings abound with the words of the Decalogue.[7]

Now, these covenant words about their devotion to God are inscribed on parchment, enclosed in a cylinder and attached to the doorposts of the principal door in the dwelling. The case and the inscription is called the *mezuzah*. On the outside is the divine name, *Shaddai*—the Almighty! *Shaddai* is formed by three Hebrew letters—*Sh-D-Y*. The letters are hidden codes for embedded words, an acronym that stands for *Shomeyr daltot Yisraeyl,* meaning "Watchman of the doors of Israel."[8] It is placed on the right side of the doorway in the upper third, eye level, and is often written in such a way that the name itself can be seen upon entering or exiting through a special slit in the cylinder. This name references God as "the Guardian of the dwellings of Israel." Here is the primitive idea of the threshold covenant, the door doubling as a sacred space, a kind of altar. When a conservative Jew passes the mezuzah, he touches the divine name with the finger of his right hand, puts that finger to his mouth and kisses it. He utters a prayer, often in Hebrew, "The Lord shall preserve your going out and your coming in from this time

---

[7] *The Jewish Study Bible*, 381.

[8] Barney Kasdan, *God's Appointed Customs* (Baltimore: Messianic Jewish, 1996) 91.

forth, and even forevermore" (Psalm 121:8). When he leaves for business he touches the mezuzah and utters, "God, I shall go out and prosper!"[9]

By depositing the Law at the door, Israel did two things. They moved clearly away from pagan notions of the threshold covenant. The favor of God was not merely about a sacred space—the doorway—but about sacred living. That new way of life was itself a doorway into greater favor with God. Obedience brought blessing.

Upon leaving Egypt, Israel camped in their tents and Moses in his. There was no special tabernacle, no tent for Yahweh. He was not yet central to the camp. However, prior to the construction of the special Tabernacle that would host God's presence was the erection of a tent in which Moses met with God. This prayer tent was set apart by the divine presence at its doorway. Here Israel first encountered the glory of God that would afterward mark the special structure called the Tabernacle of the Lord. The Tent of Meeting—where Moses met with God—had a threshold marked by divine presence.[10]

When Korah rebelled with 250 others, fire came out from before the Lord and consumed them (Numbers 16:35). The next day did not bring repentance, but more rebellion. A plague broke out among the people. The cloud of God's glory stood visibly over the Tent

---

[9] Trumbull, 63.

[10] James Strong, *The Tabernacle of Israel* (Grand Rapids: Kregel, 1987) 11.

of Meeting. Moses instructed Aaron to hastily take fire and incense and run among the people to stop the plague. In this moment, Aaron "stood between the dead and the living; so the plague was stopped" (v. 48). All the while, Moses stood at the threshold of the Tent of Meeting—the place of covenant.

Other ancients sacrificed animals before the door of their homes as a means of entering into a covenant with their god. In places in Africa, the blood of a sacrifice is still carried from the king on bunches of grass and sprinkled on the doorposts to avert evil. In many nations in unreached areas, charms and amulets adorn the doorways to protect the home from evil forces. In India, the firstfruits were not taken to the threshing floor, but to the threshold as a presentation to the gods of the household. So powerful was the belief in the threshold as a sacred place, sick children were brought to the threshold for cleansing and healing.[11]

Rabbinic authorities denounced the view of the mezuzah as an amulet or sacred charm. "The fools . . . fail to fulfill the mitzvah itself . . . which involves the Oneness of God and the reminder to love Him and worship Him and treat it (the mezuzah) as though it were an amulet designed to benefit them personally."[12]

The symbolism of the mezuzah is that God protects by the power of His Word, not by magic.

---

[11] Trumbull, 13, 15, 17.

[12] Kasdan, 90.

In Ireland, little more than a century ago, families would kill an animal and mark the four corners of the house with blood, then sprinkle the threshold. They would bore holes in the doorsill and plug them with paper on which they had copied sacred incantations. Horseshoes, toes up, nailed above a doorpost are connected to these attempts to protect the home and its threshold. In Pennsylvania, 100 years ago, it was common to cross the threshold of a new home carrying salt (a substitute for blood) and a Bible.[13]

High sills or thresholds are obsolete today. People trip over them. Handicap access has banished them. But in some ancient cultures, they were mandated. In Finland, the thresholds were designed high so one could not step on it, they had to step over it. The ancient Pythagoreans demanded that anyone entering a home who accidentally struck his foot on the threshold should back up and reenter the home. Treading on a threshold was taboo; it was an ill omen. To this day, the modern childish notion of not stepping on the cracks of a sidewalk has its roots in this reverence for the threshold. Sometimes sacred objects were buried under the threshold. Sacrifices were offered at the threshold.[14]

Rachel, the wife of Jacob, stole the family gods. The incident was terribly disconcerting to her father, Laban, who immediately moved to recover the idols.

---

[13] Trumbull, 19.
[14] Trumbull, 11-2.

Why? Rachel's possession of the family gods provided entitlement to the family estate.[15] "Now Laban had gone to shear his sheep, and Rachel had stolen the household idols that were her father's.... 'Why did you steal my gods?'" (Genesis 31:19, 30).

Sacred Boundary Lines

The family god, the god of the threshold, was the divine protector of the family estate. Sociologists say that out of this grew the idea of the sacred boundary line. It recalls the line drawn by God around the Garden of Eden, the lines around the forbidden trees. Every home was considered sacred. So the sacred line came to be identified with the home's entrance—the threshold. That sacred threshold was synonymous with the divine family altar. Entering a man's home without an invitation was aggression not only against him, but also against the god of the threshold. It became the boundary, a safe place, and the most sacred place for a family in the ancient world.[16]

To cross a sacred line without being invited suggested an intent to do harm to the people within. And it meant incurring the wrath of the household god, the divine protector. To deceptively modify the border marker of a family's property was also taboo. "You shall not remove your neighbor's landmark" (Deuteronomy 19:14). In fact, the

[15] Dr. Ronald G. Fanter, Cutting Edge Ministries, Box 1222 Round Lake Beach, IL 60073. E-mail: *revelationofjohn@revelationofjohn.com.* Source: *http://www.revelationofjohn.com/Threshold.html.*

[16] Fanter, *http://www.revelationofjohn.com/Threshold.html.*

removal of boundaries invited judgment: "'Cursed is the one who moves his neighbor's landmark.' And all the people shall say, 'Amen!'" (27:17).

In ancient times, a man pledged protection for his home, but he looked to his god for ultimate security. A thief might claw the back wall of a mud hut, but he would not enter the home by the door, lest he infuriate the protector of the home. Even a thief was too religious to solicit the wrath of a god. The doorway was associated with potential judgment. The high court of Turkey was at one time called the *Sublime Porte* or the *Exalted Gateway*.[17]

This is the basis for the idea of private ownership. Every man wants a peculiar place on the earth that can be called his own. That place is the house in which his family lives. The home was a gift and rightful inheritance from God. Place and possessions reach back to Eden. When a group of families shared their faith in a common God, an altar would be erected, most often in the middle of the camp. This place became the most holy place of the camp.

Most of these practices are obsolete today, and some have their roots in pagan notions. Yet, there is a sacredness about the threshold that we miss today. The home is the foundation for the church. The Tabernacle was God's tent. As Trumbull says, "A temple is only a more prominent house." The same word, *ohel*, is used for Abraham's tent and eventually for God's tent, often called the *Tabernacle*.[18] Around

---

17 Trumbull, 59.
18 Trumbull, 89-90.

it were the tents of the people. In front of the tent of God was the brass altar—the sacred fire. And in front of ancient tents was fire. More than utilitarian, it too was sacred fire before a sacred threshold. Without the home, the temple fails. It can never be a substitute for the home. It reinforces the home. It mirrors the home. God, the Father, is a model for every father. Our families are to be a part of a larger family. The holy place of God's tent moves us to make our tents holy places. And only when our tents are holy places do we honor the holy tent of God.

The Blood Covenant and the Threshold

To invoke the protection of his God, a man would enter into a blood covenant. This deity would be known to them as the God of the threshold. As soon as the blood had flowed upon the sacred threshold, that threshold deity began to protect the home and every member living within that home. The head of the house functioned as the priest of the home and the family. Being the head of the house and priest of the threshold God, it became the man's responsibility to be the divine protector of all who would enter into the protection of his home. He would be empowered by God to carry out his commission, but at the same time it was he who had the divine responsibility and accountability to stand in this office or function. It was understood that when a stranger was invited to step across the threshold to enter a man's home, he was submitting himself under the authority of that man while being within the confines of his home.[19] The idea of the blood covenant and the threshold is fused with red doorways. The Lutheran church building of my grandparents bears a bright-red door—a reference to the fact that we enter God's house by means of the blood. This is not peculiar to the Christian faith. Trumbull writes the following:

> In China, Japan, Korea, Siam, and India, a gate, or doorway, usually stands before Confucian and Buddhist and Shinto temples. . . . These doorways, in many places, are painted blood-color. They stand at the entrance of temple grounds, in front of shrines and sacred trees, and in every place associated with the native "*kami*"—or gods.[20]

When a bondman bound himself to a family in permanent servitude, his master would bring him unto God at the door, the threshold, and at the doorpost he would pierce the ear of the slave who would wear an earring as an indicator of his servitude (Exodus 21:5, 6; Deuteronomy 15:17). Here at the door, the place of covenant, he was bound to the family.[21]

The Threshold: The Gate of Heaven

If these ideas seem strange to us, we should notice how this gets transferred to heaven itself. When Jacob had his encounter with angels coming and going at Bethel, he set up a pillar. "And this stone which I have

---

[19] Fanter, *http://www.revelationofjohn.com/Threshold.html*.
[20] Trumbull, 94.
[21] Kasdan, 90.

set as a pillar shall be God's house, and of all that You give me I will surely give a tenth to You" (Genesis 28:22).

He declared that Bethel was none other than the gate of God. *Beth* means "house." *El* is the name of God. Thus, *Bethel* is the house of God. The pillar, or collection of stones, is meant to be a marker for the threshold to God's house! The word *sullam*, which is translated "ladder," is derived from *salal*, meaning to "raise up in a pile, to exalt by heaping up as in the construction of a mound or highway."[22] It is the notion of a stone altar as a marker for the heavenly threshold—but there is more. Out of this comes another covenant—the notion of the tithe. The tithe command is not a product of Jewish law. It, too, is associated with the threshold. Jacob would honor God, who had invited him to the threshold of heaven, by offering a tithe to Him.

Babel is alternately rendered *Bab-ilu*, or *Babi-ilu*—interpreted by some as "the door of God." This was the purpose of the tower—to access God! The ancient Egyptians called their sovereign head Pharaoh, or *Per-ao*, which may mean "the exalted house or gate," or even "door." Nebuchadnezzar II had set up mighty bulls of bronze and mighty snakes at the entrance to Babylon to protect the city.[23]

The Threshold and the Firstborn

Multiple notions get attached to the threshold, including another prevalent concept—the idea that

[22] Trumbull, 102.
[23] Trumbull, 93, 99.

the firstborn son belonged to the threshold god. In pagan cultures, the firstborn son was sometimes offered upon the threshold just as the sacrificial animal had previously been slain. Abraham would offer Isaac, but not on his threshold in Hebron or Beersheba. He would offer Isaac on the site that would later be the location of David's Tabernacle, and ultimately, the Temple of Solomon. There, God would provide His own lamb and make the pagan sacrifices obsolete. There, God would offer a prophetic picture of the One who would come to renew the ultimate threshold covenant, to create a new family in the earth—Christ, the Lamb of God. This threshold God of Abraham, whose name is *Jehovah Jireh* ("God will provide"), would become the God of Isaac, Jacob and all the tribes.

God would continue to claim the firstborn, not for sacrifice, but for service: "Consecrate to Me all the firstborn, whatever opens the womb among the children of Israel, both of man and beast; it is Mine" (Exodus 13:2). And God would give a promise to Abraham: "Your descendants shall possess the gate of their enemies" (Genesis 22:17). Jesus would later declare to his seed, "The gates of Hades shall not prevail against [you]" (Matthew 16:18). So powerful is the covenant we have with God that nothing hatched in hell's covenant laboratory—no scheme, no plot, no power of any god—can prevail against the house of the Lord with its secure threshold.

The Threshold: The Place of Renewal

When Israel was in a crisis, they worshiped the golden calf made by Aaron in the absence of Moses. It was to the threshold of the camp that Moses called the men to reaffirm their covenant with Yahweh. "Then Moses stood in the entrance of the camp, and said, 'Whoever is on the Lord's side—come to me!' And all the sons of Levi gathered themselves together to him" (Exodus 32:26).

And when Israel complained about the manna and angered God, Moses went to meet with the Lord and every man stood in the place of covenant for his own home. "Then Moses heard the people weeping throughout their families, everyone at the door of his tent; and the anger of the Lord was greatly aroused; Moses also was displeased" (Numbers 11:10).

Sacrifices were offered at the doorway of the Tabernacle. "If his offering is a burnt sacrifice...he shall offer it of his own free will at the door of the tabernacle of meeting before the Lord" (Leviticus 1:3).

Sacrifices were to be offered only to God.

> They shall no more offer their sacrifices to demons, after whom they have played the harlot. This shall be a statute forever for them throughout their generations. Also you shall say to them, "Whatever man of the house of Israel, or of the strangers who dwell among you, who offers a burnt offering or sacrifice, and does not bring it to the door of the tabernacle of meeting, to offer it to the Lord; that man shall be cut off from among his people" (17:7-9).

The Aaronic priesthood was consecrated at the threshold of the tent of the Tabernacle. At this threshold, the glory of the Lord descended. While the people would hide within their own tents, watching from their own doorways, Moses would encounter God's presence.

The Threshold: A Place of Life and Death

After Absalom was dead, David returned to the gate, the doorway to the capital of the nation (2 Samuel 19:8). Zedekiah, king of Judah, was in the gate when Ebed-Melech made his appeal in behalf of Jeremiah (Jeremiah 38:7-9). Daniel's position in the Babylonian kingdom is described as "in the gate of the king" (Daniel 2:49). The nation was called to establish "justice in the gate" (Amos 5:15) and to "execute the judgment of truth and peace in your gates" (Zechariah 8:16, KJV). A good man was one who was said to "reprove in the gate" (see Isaiah 29:21).

David sang, "A day in Your courts is better than a thousand elsewhere!" He declared that he would rather be a doorkeeper in the house of the Lord than to dwell in the tents of the wicked (see Psalm 84:10). The word *doorkeeper* means "to sit on the threshold."[24]

Jeroboam split the kingdom after the death of Solomon. He led the northern tribes in a political and spiritual revolt. His son became ill, and the king sent his wife, wearing a disguise, to see the blind and aged prophet, Abijah, in Shiloh. She did as she was

---

[24] John Ritchie, *The Tabernacle in the Wilderness* (Grand Rapids: Kregel, 1982) 18.

Threshold was a sacred place. It was a place of covenant. That's why the tradition of carrying the Bride across the threshold

told, bearing gifts for the old prophet. When the old seer heard her footsteps, he surprised her with his sight. "Come in, wife of Jeroboam!" he declared. "Why do you pretend to be another?" (1 Kings 14:6).

The Lord had given him a word for the first family of Israel, and it was bad news:

> "Go, tell Jeroboam... 'I exalted you from among the people, and made you ruler over My people Israel... and you yet have not been as My servant David, who kept My commandments... you have done more evil than all who were before you, for you have gone and made for yourself other gods and molded images to provoke Me to anger, and have cast Me behind your back—therefore behold! I will bring disaster on the house of Jeroboam, and will cut off from Jeroboam every male in Israel, bond and free'" (vv. 7-10).

The prophet was finished. There was no more to say, except, "Arise therefore, go to your own house. When your feet enter the city, the child shall die" (v. 12). Jeroboam's wife must have risen with a knot in her stomach and journeyed home with anxiety. Was he simply a cranky old man? Delusional? "Then Jeroboam's wife arose and departed, and came to Tirzah. When she came to the threshold of the house, the child died" (v. 17).

The Threshold and the Glory

The threshold! It is not only the place of death, but of life. Not only the place of grave consequences, but of promised glory. After Israel had sinned and been banished to Babylon, Ezekiel was led to consider the restoration of the nation. He sees the glory of the Lord coming into a renewed Temple. How does God reenter and reinvigorate His house in the nation? It is over the threshold! "And the glory of the Lord came into the house by the way of the doorway looking to the east" (Ezekiel 43:4, *BBE*). The *Darby* translation puts it this way: "And the glory of Jehovah came into the house by the way of the gate whose front was toward the east."

And that Temple becomes the source of a mighty river that heals the land. Ezekiel would see:

> He brought me back to the door of the temple; and there was water, flowing from under the threshold of the temple toward the east... flowing from under the right side of the temple, south of the altar... water, running out on the right side.

> And when the man... measured... he brought me through the waters; the water came up to my ankles. Again he measured... the water came up to my knees. Again he measured... the water came up to my waist. Again he measured... and it was a river that I could not cross... too deep, water in which one must swim.

> Then he said to me: "This water flows toward the eastern region, goes down into the valley, and enters the sea. When it reaches the sea, its waters are healed.... Wherever the rivers go,

> [everything] will live. There will be a very great multitude of fish. . . . Fishermen will stand by it from En Gedi to En Eglaim . . . spreading their nets. Their fish will be of the same kinds as the fish of the Great Sea, exceedingly many" (47:1, 2, 3-5, 8-10).

These healing waters, becoming a river, come from the threshold of God's house. There is healing here — not only for man, but for the environment itself...the fish in the sea, the trees that will grow along the edge of healed waters. The image of waters flowing outward that heal, out from a temple door, are immediately seen in the words of Jesus: "Out of his heart will flow rivers of living water" (John 7:38).

The Threshold and the True God

When the Philistines thought they had captured the ark of God, they placed it as a trophy in the temple to Dagon. But when they returned in the morning, the idol had fallen before the ark of God's presence. Unaware of the power that they were entertaining in their temple, they stood Dagon erect again and returned to their homes that evening. The next morning revealed a sight that would shake the entire nation to its core.

> And when they arose early the next morning, there was Dagon, fallen on its face to the ground before the ark of the Lord. The head of Dagon and both the palms of its hands were broken off on the threshold; only Dagon's torso was left

of it. Therefore neither the priests of Dagon nor any who come into Dagon's house tread on the threshold of Dagon in Ashdod to this day (1 Samuel 5:4, 5).

The picture is compelling. On the first morning, it appears that the god has fallen as if helpless or in worship before the ark of the Lord. But on the second morning, it is as if he became animated and attempted to flee his own temple only to die over his own threshold.

In this moment, Yahweh claimed the temple of Dagon for Himself. He made it clear even to the Philistines that He was the only true God. Capturing the ark and defeating Israel led them to believe they had captured Israel's God. Not so! Israel fell before them, but not Israel's God. God will not and cannot be defeated by the failure of His people. He crashes the temples of the pagan gods all by Himself. He strikes fear into the hearts of nations. He brings Ashdod to the threshold of its temple with fear. He forces them to reject their own fallen god as powerless. At the threshold of their pagan temple, the nation trembles before the only living and true God.

When Elijah challenged Israel, he asked how long they would halt between two opinions. One paraphrase of 1 Kings 18:21 is more dramatic: "How long will ye leap over both thresholds?" (that is, worship both Baal and Yahweh).[25]

---

[25] *http://www.jewishencyclopedia.com*—article on "Threshold."

Jesus the Threshold

When Israel established a Temple in the place of the Tabernacle, there were special keepers of the door. They were called *porters* (KJV) of the threshold (see 2 Kings 22:4; 1 Chronicles 9:22; 2 Chronicles 23:4; Jeremiah 35:4).[26]

Jesus declared, "I am the door" (John 10:9).

He is the true Keeper of our homes, the Gateway to God the Father, and through Him we enter the Father's family and come under the Father's protection. He is the Bridegroom of the church, His bride.

Within this new covenant family, there is protection and safety. There is comfort and blessing. There is promise and provision. Beyond it, uncertainty and judgment exist. Peter, understanding much more of the threshold's connection with covenant, must have shuttered. He had been warned about denying Christ, but he had folded under the pressure. Jesus had told him that a rooster would crow as a sign of his betrayal. Notice the place of Peter when he reached the final denial: "But he said, I have no knowledge of him, or of what you are saying: and he went out into the doorway; and there came the cry of a cock" (Mark 14:68, *BBE*).

Is it just a coincidence that his denial comes at the threshold and with the simultaneous crowing of the rooster? Peter was crossing a dangerous line, but Jesus declared that He was praying for him. Thank God for grace.

---

[26] *http://www.jewishencyclopedia.com*—article on "Threshold."

A proper thief would enter a home from some way other than the door. By not crossing over the threshold, he might incur the wrath of the owner, but he sought to avoid the greater wrath of God. Jesus alludes to this practice among thieves, but commentators generally either do not understand or simply choose not to expound upon these things. "Most assuredly, I say to you, he who does not enter the sheepfold by the door, but climbs up some other way, the same is a thief and a robber" (John 10:1).

Jesus himself did not violate the threshold. He said, "Behold, I stand at the door and knock. If anyone hears My voice and opens the door, I will come in to him and dine with him, and he with Me" (Revelation 3:20). This refers to the partaking of the covenant meal. When we invite Christ into our lives as Lord, He crosses the sacred threshold of our hearts. We submit ourselves to Him.

> Of how much worse punishment, do you suppose, will he be thought worthy who has trampled the Son of God underfoot, counted the blood of the covenant by which he was sanctified a common thing, and insluted the Spirit of grace? (Hebrews 10:29).

We should not be in a hurry to enter through a door just because that door has been suddenly opened before us. Not every door is of God. Doorways can lead to sinful behavior.

Some temples were equipped with a false door believed to lead to the underworld. It was properly called a false door because there was nothing on the other side. Jesus spoke about the "strait gate." The gate was narrow and restricted, suggestive of the required submission to the threshold God who in this case is clearly Christ himself. "Enter ye in at the strait gate: for wide is the gate, and broad is the way, that leadeth to destruction, and many there be which go in thereat" (Matthew 7:13, KJV).

The wide gate leads to destruction, not merely of physical extinction; it is a plunge into hell.

Adam passed through the door that led him to death. His desire to return to life, held only by God, was prevented by the cherubim who stood at the door leading back to the Paradise. The threshold covenant marked the boundary and limitation of man's access to God.

> "I know your works. See, I have set before you an open door, and no man can shut it; for you have a little strength, have kept My word, and have not denied My name" (Revelation 3:8).

Because of Jesus, that door is now an open door that no being can shut. "Jesus answered and said to them, 'This is the work of God, that you believe in Him whom He sent'" (John 6:29).

In ancient times, the invited guests to formal banquets presented their tablets or cards to a servant posted at the doorway. His role was to allow the invited to pass over the threshold and disallow those whose invitations were invalid. When the last guest had arrived, the master of the house closed the door. No matter how urgent the appeal to enter, after the door was closed, no one else was allowed to cross the threshold.[27]

Do you have your invitation? Are you ready for the Marriage Supper?

The culminating act in a Jewish wedding is the *nissuin,* based on the verb *nasa,* meaning "to carry." The bride would wait for the groom to arrive to carry her away to their new home. She knew the approximate time would be near the conclusion of their yearlong betrothal. But the exact time of the groom's arrival was a mystery, which added to the element of surprise. The father of the groom gave the approval for the *nissuin* to begin.[28]

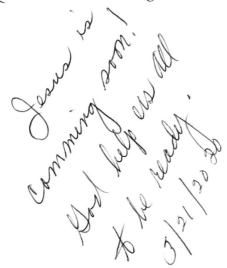

[27] James M. Freeman, *Manners and Customs of the Bible* (Peabody, MA: Hendrickson, 1988) 379.
[28] Kasdan, 51.

MOVEMENT FIVE

Entertaining God and Influencing Cities

Genesis 18:20-33

And the Lord said, "Because the outcry against Sodom and Gomorrah is great, and because their sin is very grave, I will go down now and see whether they have done altogether according to the outcry against it that has come to Me; and if not, I will know."

Then the men turned away from there and went toward Sodom, but Abraham still stood before the Lord. And Abraham came near and said, "Would You also destroy the righteous with the wicked? Suppose there were fifty righteous within the city; would You also destroy the place and not spare it for the fifty righteous that were in it? Far be it from You to do such a thing as this, to slay the righteous with the wicked, so that the righteous should be as the wicked; far be it from You! Shall not the Judge of all the earth do right?"

So the Lord said, "If I find in Sodom fifty righteous within the city, then I will spare all the place for their sakes."

Then Abraham answered and said, "Indeed now, I who am but dust and ashes have taken it upon myself to speak to the Lord: Suppose there were five less than the fifty righteous; would You destroy all of the city for lack of five?" So He said, "If I find there forty-five, I will not destroy it."

And he spoke to Him yet again and said, "Suppose there should be forty found there?"

So He said, "I will not do it for the sake of forty."

Then he said, "Let not the Lord be angry, and I will speak: Suppose thirty should be found there?"

So He said, "I will not do it if I find thirty there."

And he said, "Indeed now, I have taken it upon myself to speak to the Lord: Suppose twenty should be found there?"

So He said, "I will not destroy it for the sake of twenty."

Then he said, "Let not the Lord be angry, and I will speak but once more: Suppose ten should be found there?"

And He said, "I will not destroy it for the sake of ten." So the Lord went His way as soon as He had finished speaking with Abraham; and Abraham returned to his place.

The Story of Dawson Trotman and the Navigators

In 1931, a 25-year-old lumberyard worker named Dawson Trotman engaged God for 40 days of prayer. From his youthful days as a liar, gambler and pool shark, he had made a remarkable turn. He now rose each morning, placing his life in the hands of God. He laid himself freshly on the altar at the start of each new day—giving the rest of his life to God. He prayed that God would use him to reach the nations for Christ, one person at a time.

Does anything concrete develop of such times of prayer? At the end of the 40 days, he was praying over maps of the United States and then the world. In his pursuit of God, he had ended up in prayer for the nations! Presumptuous for a 25-year-old? Perhaps. His plan for world impact was far too simple—disciple one person until he or she had successfully made a disciple of another.

A few years later, Dawson would create a network to accomplish this goal. When World War II started, his goal was to have *a key man* on every Naval vessel in service. With the U.S. Navy all over the world, Dawson's disciple-makers would also be all over the world. During the winter of 1945, he gathered others to pray for those they personally knew who were in military action. He had a list of hundreds of men in service. The network was off and sailing. And every week, at 5 a.m., Dawson rallied prayer support for evangelism among the nations through the winter and into spring. Each week, new names were added to the prayer list. The group began to pray, not only for the servicemen, but also for the countries where they served. Whole regions became the focus of prayer—Southeast Asia, the countries of Europe.

Six years later, Dawson reported "astonishing an-swers to our prayers for servicemen." In the countries that had been intentionally prayed for—countries in and near the battle zones—there was now a full-time evangelism worker in the 15 or more countries that had been the focus of prayer. In at least six nations, more than one missionary was present. "And that was within six years of the time when we were praying so earnestly." It was no coincidence. Prayer had given influence over nations.[1]

The code letters for his quiet time were HWLW—"His Word the Last Word."[2] He routinely walked to a knoll at the end of his street of which his biographer says, "Here he spent precious hours alone, praying aloud, singing praise to the Lord, quoting Scriptures of

[1] Robert Boyd Munger, *Leading From the Heart* (Colorado Springs: Intervarsity, 1995) 96-8.

[2] Betty Lee Skinner, *Daws: The Story of Dawson Trotman, Founder of the Navigators* (Grand Rapids: Zondervan, 1974) 103.

promise and challenge that flooded his mind—now wrestling in urgent prayer, now pacing the hillside in silence."[3]

Dawson believed God blessed the person, not the institution. Men procure the favor of God for institutions, for cities and nations. Dawson Trotman did. In a short season, God had moved a young man praying over maps to create a worldwide organization—the Navigators![4] Over 4,000 Navigators from 63 nationalities now serve the world, discipling 110 nations and 214 people groups with 161 different languages—one person at a time.[5]

Even his death was a metaphor. He died after rescuing a young girl from drowning. At his funeral, Billy Graham declared, "I think Dawson Trotman has personally touched more lives [for Christ's sake] than anybody that I have ever known." The young man who at 25 entertained God over the maps of the world influenced nations.

[3] Skinner, 257.
[4] *http://www.willvaus.com/god_s_person.*
[5] *http://www.navigators.org/us/view/one-to-one_mr/2005/ Winter% 202005/Inside%20This%20Issue/God's%20 Instrument.*

11

INFLUENCE OVER
CITIES!

There is a pattern in the Scripture. God waits to judge. He doesn't rush to judgment because He is slow to anger and long in mercy.

F.B. Meyer says:

> He walks our streets day and night. He patrols our thoroughfares, marking everything, missing nothing. He glides unmasked into our most sacred privacy; for all things are naked and open to [His] eyes. . . . He is prepared, nay, eager to give us the benefit of any excuse.[1]

He waits to awaken intercessors! "In prayer the Church has received power to rule the world. The Church is always the little flock. But if it would stand together on its knees, it would dominate world politics—from the prayer room."[2] *so true*

---

[1] F.B. Meyer, *Abraham, God's Friend* (Westchester, IL: Good News, 1962) 47.
[2] O. Hallesby, Prayer (Minneapolis: Augsburg, 1959) 158.

A few miles from Hebron, in the area of Ziph, the landscape changes dramatically. Two routes lead down the rocky gorges into a valley dropping precipitously more than 3,000 feet above sea level to 1,300 feet below it. The view is staggering. From the edges of these Judean hills, one can see on a clear day all of the Dead Sea Valley. Looking across the Dead Sea to the southeast edge, the cities of the plain were visible.

Waking Up Intercession

The two angels moved toward Sodom and Gomorrah, but the Angel of the Lord remained with Abraham. His destination was never the cities of the plain. He came to wake up something in Abraham—and He was not finished with that task. Abraham apparently walked with Him toward Sodom.

With Sodom and Gomorrah in view, an extraordinary exchange takes place. Abraham boldly asked, "Will You destroy the righteous with the wicked?" He had in mind his nephew, Lot. Twenty years had passed since Lot left him. His only contacts with his nephew had been to rescue him. He couldn't forget him. Here is grace. Despite the crooked and self-centered dealings of Lot, Abraham would not stand idly with Lot in harm's way. He did not allow the negative encounters with Lot to stifle his loving concern. What we do tells on us when we hold in our hands the destiny of someone who has hurt or harmed us. Abraham laid aside any personal issues with Lot.

This is called the first solemn prayer on record in the Bible; and it is a prayer to spare Sodom. Abraham prayed earnestly that Sodom be spared if a few righteous persons were found there. Come and learn from Abraham what compassion we should feel for sinners and how earnestly we should pray for them. Not even with Noah do we have such an intense exchange with God. Here Abraham steps between God and the souls of Sodom. He becomes a prophetic type of Christ. He is in the role every intercessor must play. He steps into the path of judgment. This is the essence of intercession—standing between.

Six times he countered God, and six times God granted his petition. When he struck grace, he persisted in prayer. Was he drawing mercy from an unwilling God? No, it was not Abraham who was moving God, it was God who was drawing Abraham into his burden for the sinful world, evidenced by these cities of the plain.[3]

This was God's purpose—to wake up the intercessor in Abraham. Out of him would come the intercessory nation. God would plant Israel on the land bridge that connected the three continents of the ancient world. Any land empire that sought to dominate the world would have to march through this continental corridor. In one sense, God did not give Abraham and the Jewish people a nation, He gave them a hallway.

---

[3] Meyer, 49.

Why? He wanted them to stand between Himself and the nations, to be the intercessors for the earth. They would be prophets on one hand, declaring the truths of God, and priests on the other, reconciling men to God. He wanted Israel to be the model nation, an inclusive people. Through Israel, the whole earth was to be blessed and reconciled to God. But it did not happen.

In Exodus 19:5, 6, standing at the foot of Mount Sinai, God declared His purpose. He had called Israel to be what Abraham had been before—an intercessor. They were to be a whole nation of intercessors, a kingdom of priests, but they turned down the job. They opted for a layer of special priests between them and God. He was too "wild" for them. They preferred the quiet life to the sight of fire on the top of Sinai and God's trumpet-like voice screaming in siren fashion. It was too unnerving.

Indirect relationships are never as secure or fulfilling as direct relationships. The mission failed. Israel did not develop into the intercessor nation God had intended for them to become. They backslid. They divided and committed adultery with other gods. Ten northern tribes were carried into Assyria, never to return. The two southern tribes were whisked off to Babylon. And the lights go out in Jerusalem, God's city on a hill.

A Nation Reborn

After 70 years, mercy met its mission, and God's purpose was reclaimed. Only a remnant returned, about a tenth, according to Isaiah 6. Isaiah declared the purpose of their reconstitution: "You shall be named the priests of the Lord" (61:6). Isaiah directs them with this appeal:

> Listen to Me, you who follow after righteousness, you who seek the Lord: Look to the rock from which you were hewn, and to the hole of the pit from which you were dug. Look to Abraham your father, and to Sarah who bore you; for I called him alone, and blessed him and increased him (51:1, 2).

To chart their new course meant going back beyond the days of David, beyond the Exodus, to the great patriarch himself, Abraham. In him is the clue to why God blessed the nation. He was a friend of God.

Now we are back at God's original purpose— creating a nation of intercessors. But it didn't happen. Again, they created a layer of holy people between God and the common man.

Jesus came and assessed the situation. His people had not stood between the nations and God with an inclusive posture. They had not dispensed the favor and grace of God, they had become the exclusive recipients of God's goodness. They had shut up the kingdom for themselves. He picked up the scroll of Isaiah and read, declaring His purpose to create a kingdom of priests. For more than three years, He labored with 12 disciples. He poured Himself into them. They operated as a team of priestly ministers to the people, but the nation was unmoved. The establishment hardened against Him. And Jesus gave them a sad report: "Your kingdom will not continue!" They missed their calling to be a nation of intercessors for the nations.

The Church—Called to Intercession

So Israel is temporarily set aside, not abandoned, but God will now accomplish His purposes through "whosoever will." He raises up the church and pours out His Spirit on the Day of Pentecost. The whole world, representatively, is gathered together. Peter offered an explanation of what they were witnessing with the tongues of fire. He declared, "Jesus, whom you crucified, the One you did not entertain very well, rose from the dead, ascended to heaven, and is seated on the throne of David, and has sent forth this message—you must repent!" (see Acts 2:22-39).

The Spirit-filled, Christ-exalting church now stands between the enthroned Jesus and the world. Here is intercession, both the prophetic and the priestly. They offer the prophetic truth—sin demands repentance. Pride must be broken with humility. Arrogant actions must be terminated with the obedient act of baptism. They offer priestly love—repentance will bring forgiveness. A new community is forming in the earth. The church is where God wanted Abraham and the nation of Israel.

In the Revelation, Jesus would remind us of a task. We are to be priests to serve God (Revelation 1:6). Peter would challenge the church to be a "holy priesthood" (1 Peter 2:5). We may have pastors, but they are not our priests. We are all called to be the priests of the Lord, standing between Him and the hurting, between Him and potential judgment, between Him and whole cities—perhaps whole nations.

This is the destiny of the church—to stand between kings and the King of kings, between nations and the kingdom of God, to be agents of truth and love.

> The ministry of the church is not merely preaching . . . it is . . . to bring the will of heaven to the earth. Prayer is not as small and insignificant as some may think. It is not something that is dispensable. Prayer is a work. Prayer is the church saying to God, "God, we want your will." Prayer is the church knowing God's heart and opening its mouth to ask for what is in God's heart. If the church does not do this, it does not have much use in the earth.[4]

Another Failure

But the church followed the pattern of Israel, eventually installing a layer of priests between the people and God. Thus, in the Reformation, Luther sounds the theme again. God wants to establish "the priesthood of all believers." Unfortunately, we have understood this in the narrow and personal way of talking to God merely for ourselves, about ourselves. Priesthood

---

[4] Watchman Nee, *The Prayer Ministry of the Church* (Anaheim, CA: Living Stream Ministry, 1993) 13.

has more cosmic purposes than that. The church, and every believer in it, are called to stand between others and God—families, couples, nations, cities, missionaries, corporations, schools, hospitals, legal institutions, the disadvantaged, the poor, the hungry, the down-and-out, the up-and-out, the drug dealer, the drug user, the prostitute, the pimp, the oppressor, the oppressed. The church is called to stand between these people and God, not in a way that separates or provides a screen, but in a way that seeks to reconcile. We are called to be peacemakers, agents of healing in broken relationships.

Now, 500 years after the Reformation, we appear to be no closer to the completion of this mission. Our churches offer entertainment and inspirational moral talks to disengaged people who perceive themselves as followers of the radical Christ. The church is largely irrelevant to the culture around us. We are not the peacemakers at the community table. Tragically, we are sometimes the agitating party. We have shut up the Kingdom for ourselves. People shop for churches that preach a version of the gospel they prefer. We privatize our faith and miss the call to a corporate mission.

Our response is to give money that soothes our conscience and releases us from critical personal involvement. We have fled the inner city and relocated our churches in the safe suburbs away from crime and poverty. We see no connection between the location of our church buildings and mission. We do not seek strategic locations having considered their mission possibility. We seek convenient locations, irrelevant to their neighborhoods, having only considered personal expediency. It is all about us. Rather than running to our position as intercessors to stand between the disenfranchised and a missionary God, we have retreated to the safety of our comfortable homes.

It is time for another reformation!

Reforming the Church

We live in an increasingly pagan age. We do not weep over the death of absolutes in the face of relativism. Our revisionist history has scripted out the Christian roots of our nation. We are not appalled at the promotion of religious pluralism under the banner of multiculturalism. Christianity is increasingly set aside. Among the other gods being explored, only the name of Jesus is banned.

The climate of religious paganism is not new to the church. Our faith is not so fragile that it will not survive. It has faced such opposition before, and it has conquered it. "Three hundred years after the beginning of Christ's public ministry, the church brought the Roman Empire to its knees in worship of the Redeemer."[5]

How did they do it? In the New Testament era, when the Empire rose up with force against the church and killed James and imprisoned Peter with the intention of killing him the next day, the church fell to its knees.

---

[5] Harold Lindsell, *The New Paganism* (San Francisco: Harper and Row, 1987) 22.

In the inner cell, surrounded by 16 prisoners and bound on either side by two guards, Peter walked out. No one saw him. No one stopped him. Chains fell off. Gates supernaturally opened. While all of this happened, the church was on its knees, fervently praying.[6]

The pagans outside are not our problem. Our problem is pagans inside.

The mention of the Book of Malachi usually anticipates the topic of tithing, but Malachi writes about a bigger problem. Only in the land for a few years, the spiritual life of the resurrected nation was languishing.

The people lacked integrity. They offered crippled animals on the altar. Since the animal was going to die anyway, or be wasted in the burnt offering, they gave sick, blind, crippled animals to God and kept the best for themselves. The practice polluted their worship. They had a diminished view of God. "I am a great King!" Jehovah cries out in response to their practices (1:14). A lack of respect for God is revealed in the way they treated the disadvantaged around them. They paid a less-than-livable wage, creating a poverty sector, something God had warned about (3:5). Divorce was rampant, indicating how men were dishonoring their wives (2:13, 14).

Bill Hybels calls them a cheating culture because they cheated God, the poor and their wives. And then

---

[6] Ronald Dunn, *Don't Just Stand There, Pray Something: The Incredible Power of Intercessory Prayer* (Nashville: Thomas Nelson, 1992) 217.

they turned to God and dared to ask for a blessing, as if blind to the inconsistency of their lives. "You weep and wail because he no longer pays attention to your offerings or accepts them with pleasure from your hands. You ask, 'Why?' It is because the Lord is acting as the witness between you and the wife of your youth, because you have broken faith with her, though she is your partner, the wife of your marriage covenant" (vv. 13, 14, *NIV*).[7]

Leanne Payne warns against "Christianized secular psychologies that assign innocence to sin and evil. Sin and evil in a person or situation are renamed, with evil being called good and good being called evil. God and evil are thereby . . . reconciled." Such systems are "pagan and Gnostic." She charges that "New Age neognosticism is being spread throughout the church today, covered with a veneer of psychology (mostly Jungian) terminology."

The result is that people are charting their own spiritual courses using Biblical principles and Christian terminology and leaving out "a transforming moment with God that brings the soul into union with a transcendent Holy Other."

So the "transforming moment" is not with God. It is "union with themselves!" It is "self-discovery!" They are not guided by something outside themselves, bigger than themselves—they use outside sources and insights to interpret "the images of their

---

[7] Bill Hybels, *Too Busy Not to Pray* (Downers Grove, IL: Intervarsity, 1988) 89-90.

own heart." Dreams, visions, images, feelings are all subjective. It is an inner turning, "a subjectivity that is ego-related." It is religious narcissism where "the self becomes god." Their own story is more important than the greater story in which they are a small part—God's story. The old paganism is born again in the modern church.[8]

[8] Leanne Payne, *Listening Prayer* (Grand Rapids: Baker, 1994) 89.

12

JOINING JESUS IN
PRAYER!

The only picture we have of Christ's activity now is that He is interceding (Romans 8:34; Hebrews 7:24, 25). He is seated at the right hand of the Father, but He is still working. His earthly task is finished, but His ministry still affects the earth. He is praying for us. It is to His current role as intercessor that He calls us. It is our highest obligation and greatest privilege. In it is our greatest power and deepest capacity for influence. To be like Jesus is to be an intercessor. To be in unity with Jesus is to join Him in prayer for the world around us. To emote like Jesus is to weep over cities. This is the role to which He has called every Christian. His reign is extended first through intercessory prayer. On our knees we fulfill our royal function as a kingdom of priests (1 Peter 2:5, 9). Through our praying, Christ prays.

Through our intercession, He secures victories and distributes blessing. Through our intercession, He breaks strongholds. Through our intercession, He opens the eyes of the spiritually blind and releases them from the bondage of sin. Through our intercession, He rules the nations. The kings are in His hands (Proverbs 21:1). The reigns to their hearts are held by intercession.

God the Son is praying. And God the Spirit is praying (Romans 8:26; 1 Corinthians 14:14). The intercessory Trinity is not complete until you and I join with the Son and Spirit in petitioning the Father.

> The praying Christ is on the throne of heaven, face-to-face with the Father. But we weak, finite human beings, saved by the grace of God, are given the almost unbelievable privilege of reaching our hands to heaven and also touching God's throne. Then the prayer team God has ordained is complete. In some sacred sense we share with Christ in mediating God's blessings. In some sacred sense, God blesses the world through our prayer. Prayer enables us to touch God's throne with one hand and the needy world with the other.[1]

God must be true to the integrity of His own nature of holiness. It is His desire that we, with full understanding of His righteous heart, plead for mercy in behalf of the nations. We are not asking for holiness

---

[1] Wesley Duewel, *Touch the World Through Prayer* (Grand Rapids. Zondervan, 1986) 63.

to be subverted, but for mercy to be extended in order that some might be saved. We are asking that a city might learn how valuable the righteous are who live among them—how the presence of small amounts of salt and light in the midst of corruption and darkness makes a difference to God. "For Zion's sake I will not keep silent, for Jerusalem's sake I will not remain quiet, till her righteousness shines out like the dawn, her salvation like a blazing torch" (Isaiah 62:1, *NIV*).

Where will our God be heard if He will not be silent? Note verses 6 and 7: "I have posted watchmen on your walls, O Jerusalem; they will never be silent day or night. You who call on the Lord, give yourselves no rest, and give him no rest till he establishes Jerusalem and makes her the praise of the earth" (*NIV*).

This is the place occupied by James, the half brother of Jesus, who spent countless hours on his knees interceding for Israel's blindness and the strength of the church of Jerusalem in his charge. When he died, after being pushed from the pinnacle of the Temple and then clubbed to death, his knees were said to be like camels' knees, thickly calloused as a result of the hours he had spent in prayer. This is the place in which Savonarola stood to pray down revival in 15th-century Italy. This is the place in which David Brainerd frequently knelt as a missionary to the American Indians. The is the place from which "Praying Hyde" lifted his voice for India's salvation. This is the place between, the place designed for the intercessor.[2]

[2] Duewel, *Touch the World Through Prayer*, 12.

[handwritten] ✓ Friday 3/30 20 Italy is hit the worst with the Corona Virus. please Lord send revival again.

Samuel Chadwick made this observation: "There is a marked absence of travail. There is much phrasing, but little pleading. Prayer has become a soliloquy instead of a passion. The powerlessness of the church has no other explanation.... To be prayerless is to be both passionless and powerless."[3]

The Triangle of Intercession

In Luke 11, we find the classic picture of the intercessory triangle—the one in need, the one who can meet the need, and the man in the middle. All around us are people in need, with needs that we cannot humanly satisfy. Above us is God, who can meet any or all of these needs. We are the community of intercessors in the middle. In prayer, we engage God to meet the needs of others.

The intercessor in Dr. Luke's story sacrifices his sleep to meet the need of a friend. He risks his friendship, by asking his neighbor to feed the stranger. The key is the man in the middle. He was not hungry. His guest was famished, but he acted as if he were the hungry one. This is intercession—owning the need, praying as if you were the one being prayed for. The intercessor, in prayer, takes the place of the man in need. This is the cross.[4] Help me, Lord!

[3] Quoted by Wesley Duewel, *Mighty Prevailing Prayer* (Grand Rapids: Zondervan, 1990) 212.

[4] Ronald Dunn, *Don't Just Stand There, Pray Something: The Incredible Power of Intercessory Prayer* (Nashville: Thomas Nelson, 1992) 86.

In verse 8, Jesus sums up the story of the friend in need: "I say to you, though he will not rise and give him because he is his friend, yet because of his persistence he will rise and give him as many as he needs."

The word *friend* is loaded with warmth and affection. It is a term of endearment. But strangely, the relationship is not enough by itself. Passion and insistence need to be added to the recipe. *Importunity is an Old English word*. It means more than persistence, it is "shameless persistence." The friend in the middle refuses to accept the social restraints of niceness. He will not be embarrassed by the clamor he is causing at the midnight hour. He will not be silenced. He will not go quietly in the night. He will accept no humiliation for waking up the neighborhood. He is stubbornly bent on getting this need met.[5]

Wesley Duewel reminds us of the following needs:

> God's cause creeps forward timidly and slowly when there are more organizers than agonizers, more workers than prevailing prayer warriors. We need prayer warriors who have seen the heart of God, who have experienced the power and glory of the Cross, who know the Bible meaning and significance of the day of Judgment, heaven and hell. We need prayer warriors who feel the slavery, the absence of any eternal hope, and the doom of the unsaved; who feel the transforming power, joy, and glory from Christ of the saved. We need prayer war-

[handwritten margin note: oh God, Help me to be one!]

---

[5] Dunn, 76.

riors who pray as though God is God and as
though Satan is Satan.

God seeks people to prevail in prayer. It is His
ordained means to move the world toward
righteousness and the people of the world
toward salvation.[6]

During the Welsh Revival, strangers entered the vil-
lages unaware of the movement of God and fell under
deep conviction. They would drop all plans and seek
out a minister to pray for them. Boats coming near the
shore, unaware of the movement of prayer, would
find their crews smitten with a sudden awareness of
their sins. Before the ship docked in the harbor, every
man on board would have made peace with God.
During the ministry of Finney, it is reported that he
walked down the street, into factories, and people
would be moved to prayer and repentance.[7] In the
New York Awakening of 1858, ships coming into the
harbor reported an awareness of God's presence miles
before they came into the waters around Long Island.

We need another great awakening—an "atmo-
spheric revival" where the presence of God is so
thick that even the unbelievers find His pervasive
presence inescapable.

Dick Eastman recalls in his book *Beyond Imagination*
that just over 100 years ago, A.T. Pierson and D.L.
Moody conspired to challenge the church to finish
its obligation to the Great Commission.[8] In 1885, at

[6] Duewel, *Mighty Prevailing Prayer,* 23.
[7] Dunn, 232.

a conference in Northfield, Massachusetts, Pierson presented the vision for reaching every person in every nation by the year 1900. Pierson reckoned that only 10 million Christians of the 400 million available would have to be mobilized. If each of them would reach only 100 people over the next 15 years, the task would be complete. So moved was Moody that in the course of Pierson's challenge, he leaped to his feet and enthusiastically asked the crowd, "How many of you believe this can be done?" The crowd cheered. A committee was appointed. A document was prepared. But 10 years later, Pierson would la-ment, "We're compelled to give up the hope."

The collapse of the mission could be traced to two faults. Individuals were excited about the mission, but the corporate church itself never owned the vision or developed strategic plans to fulfill it. Equally significant, prayer support for the vision was never mobilized.[9]

"God has a wonderful plan by which you can have worldwide influence," declares Wesley Duewel in the opening line of his book *Touch the World Through Prayer*. He continues:

> Through prayer you can accompany any missionary to remote reaches of the earth ... walk

[8] Dick Eastman, *Beyond Imagination* (Grand Rapids: Chosen Books—a division of Baker, 1997) 269-70.

[9] Todd Johnson and Ralph Winter, "Will We Fail Again?" (A compilation of previously printed works edited by Rick Wood) *Mission Frontiers* bulletin (Pasadena, CA: U.S. Center for World Mission, July/August 1993) 12.

This is what you told me about when y.N.C. when first started. (handwritten margin note)

through crowded bazaars, minister in steaming jungles, feed millions of starving men, women, and children, hungry for bread for their bodies and for the Bread of Life.

Through prayer you can contribute to the ministry of any pastor or evangelist in a church or gospel hall anywhere in the world. Many a time I have felt that through prayer I was at the side of some man or woman of God.[10]

"Prayer unites puny man to Almighty God in miraculous partnership. It is the most noble and most essential ministry God gives to His children—but it is the most neglected."[11] It is asking divine omnipotence to work through yielded human weakness.[12] With such a resource we should pray more. Oswald Chambers exhorted, "Never say you will pray about a thing: pray about it."[13]

Duewel says, "The Holy Spirit was given at Pentecost, not to keep the church blessed and comfortable, but to make the church invincible."[14]

The Angel of the Lord coached Abraham out of his camp, away from his tent. They probably stood on a mountain ridge overlooking the valley below. Across the Dead Sea the cities of the plain were clearly visible. Abraham pleaded for 50 righteous

---

[10] Duewel, *Touch the World Through Prayer*, 11.

[11] P.J. Johnstone, *Operation World—A Handbook for World Intercession* (Bromley-Kent, England: STL, 1978) 15.

[12] D. Edmond Hiebert, *Working With God Through Intercessory Prayer* (Greenville, SC: Bob Jones UP, 1991) 22.

[13] Vernon McLellan, *Thoughts That Shaped the Church* (Wheaton, IL: Tyndale, 2000) 1.

[14] Duewel, *Touch the World Through Prayer*, 208.

to spare the city. Then he pleaded for 45 . . . 40. He became bolder and asked for 30; bolder yet for 20; finally, 10. He must have been amazed to find God so incredibly accommodating. It is in intercession that we draw out—for cities and nations, for individuals and families—the mercy and grace of God.

Abraham prayed and angels worked to deliver his nephew Lot.

Samuel Chadwick notes:

> There is no power like that of prevailing prayer—of Abraham pleading for Sodom, Jacob wrestling in the stillness of the night, Moses standing in the breach, Hannah intoxicated with sorrow, David heartbroken with remorse and grief, Jesus in sweat and blood. Add to this list from the records of the church your personal observation and experience, and always there is cost of passion unto blood. Such prayer prevails. It turns ordinary mortals into men of power. It brings power. It brings fire. It brings rain. It brings life. It brings God.[15]

Abraham pleaded for the nations that were about to experience destruction. Nature itself warred against the cities of the plain. The ground on which the intercessor stands is always one of conflict. Sometimes it is soaked with blood. Often it is filled with the foreboding potential of doom.

> Prayer warfare is not your begging God to help you do His will, or trying to convince God of

[15] Quoted by Lewis and Betty Drummond, *The Spiritual Woman* (Grand Rapids: Kregel, 1999) 220.

the magnitude of a need. Prayer warfare is joining Christ in driving out and defeating Satan and in setting his captives free. It is advancing against Satan's strongholds and dislodging and expelling his demon forces. Satan is a pretender, with no right to dominate and enslave the lives of those for whom Christ died. He has no right to harass and oppress people, to dupe and frighten them into submitting to him. Satan has been totally defeated at Calvary.... Prayer warfare is enforcing the victory of Calvary against Satan's deceptive schemes and defeated spirit-helpers.[16]

The Royal Dimension of Intercession

"I am but dust, and I have taken it upon myself to speak to the Almighty," Abraham pleaded (see Genesis 18:27). The words seem strange to us. We have so cheapened prayer that we have forgotten the royal dimension that it implies. In a democratic nation where we constantly level the field and undercut the hierarchy, we develop little respect for authority. There is nothing we bow before. We are increasingly sullen.

We are a "talk-back" culture. Our president is not finished speaking before a myriad of news media fills ears with their contrary opinions. In such a culture, we tend to make our God like ourselves. Our approach to Him is casual. Our confidence in Him is conditional. Our approval rating is based on His performance. And as a nation, we seem now to be shopping for another god.

---

[16] Duewel, *Touch the World Through Prayer*, 208.

Have you ever met royalty, a king or queen? It is not like anything we know in our American world. One must know how to respectfully approach royalty, how to curtsy, how to back away without stumbling or turning his or her back to royalty. Wesley Duewel says, "You must never speak first; wait until you are spoken to. You never ask royalty anything; you answer royalty. . . . In your first reply, you must add the words, 'Your Majesty.'"[17]

Abraham contested the pending judgment of Sodom. He contended with God, but he did so with humility, ever remembering that he was "but dust!"

Wesley Duewel says:

> The greatest privilege God gives to you is the freedom to approach Him at any time. You are not only authorized to speak to Him; you are invited. You are not only permitted; you are expected. God waits for you to communicate with Him. You have instant, direct access to God. God loves mankind so much, and in a very special sense His children, that He has made Himself available to you at all times.[18]

Don't miss the point. Abraham began by entertaining God—asking for nothing. His desire was to please God. In the end of this encounter, he potentially held the destiny of city-states in his hands.

Entertaining God leads to influence over cities. And through the mystery of prayer, it is as if you are trans-

---

[17] Duewel, *Touch the World Through Prayer*, 21.
[18] Duewel, *Touch the World Through Prayer*, 21.

ported to the very place for which you pray. Through prayer, you enter homes, offices, government buildings, courtrooms, secret meetings, bars and boardrooms.

In Psalm 2, a messianic psalm, we read staggering words:

> I will proclaim the decree of the Lord: He said to me, "You are my Son; today I have become your Father. Ask of me, and I will make the nations your inheritance, the ends of the earth your possession" (vv. 7, 8, *NIV*).

"Ask and I will give you the nations!" Influence over nations is clearly tied to prayer! Is this what Jesus is now asking the Father? If so, should our prayers not be more missional? Should we not be praying for kings, for the godly influence of the kingdom of God to reach into the highest realms of authority? Indeed we should.

We tend to miss the connection of the gospel with the Kingdom! It is not merely good news that we are called to preach. It is the good news of the in-breaking Kingdom. A new government is rising in the earth. There is a new King, a different kind of King, who offers an inside-out government. It was the gospel of the Kingdom that Jesus preached at the beginning of His ministry (Matthew 4:23), in the midst of His ministry (9:35), and at the end of His earthly ministry (24:14). It was about the Kingdom that He spoke to His disciples in the 40 days after His resurrection (Acts 1:3). It was about the Kingdom that Paul preached as the Book of Acts closes (28:23, 31).

Psalm 9 describes the dilemma—the nations have forgotten God (v. 17). Paul argued that they do not retain the knowledge of God (Romans 1:28). That is certainly the case with the United States. They misinterpret God's blessings as their own achievements. They fail to give Him thanks (v. 21). They are hardened by His judgments (2:5; Revelation 16:21).[19]

Paul exhorted us in this way:

> Therefore I exhort first of all that supplications, prayers, intercessions, and giving of thanks be made for all men, for kings and all who are in authority, that we may lead a quiet and peaceable life in all godliness and reverence. For this is good and acceptable in the sight of God our Savior, who desires all men to be saved and to come to the knowledge of the truth (1 Timothy 2:1-4).

In 1650, Jeremy Taylor wrote *The Rules and Exercises of Holy Living*. He offers this perspective on prayer:

> Christ hath put it [the power of prayer] into the hands of men, and the prayers of men have saved cities and kingdoms from ruin; prayer hath raised dead men to life, hath stopped the violence of fire, shut the mouths of wild beasts, altered the course of nature, caused rain in Egypt and drought in the sea. Prayer rules over all gods; it arrests the sun in its course and stays the chariot wheels of the moon; it reconciles our suffering and weak faculties with the violence of torment and the violence of persecution; it

---

[19] Duewel, *Touch the World Through Prayer*, 88.

pleases God and supplies all our need.[20]

> Prayer can obtain everything; can open the windows of heaven and shut the gates of hell; can put a holy constraint upon God, and detain an angel till he leaves a blessing; can open the treasures of rain and soften the iron ribs of rocks till they melt into a flowing river; can arrest the sun in his course, and send the winds upon our errands.[21]

Somehow, our praying for kings is related to the desire of God for the salvation of men on the planet. And notice the next phrase in 1 Timothy 2. It is tied to the role of Christ as Mediator and Intercessor: "For there is one God and one Mediator between God and men, the Man Christ Jesus, who gave Himself a ransom for all" (vv. 5, 6).

Sir Thomas Browne was an English physician in the 1600s. Listen to his declaration:

> I have resolved to pray more and pray always, to pray in all places where quietness inviteth: in the house, on the highway and on the street; and to know no street or passage in this city that may not witness that I have not forgotten God. I purpose to take occasion of praying upon the sight of any church which I may pass, that God may be worshiped there in spirit, and that souls may be saved there; to pray daily for my sick patients and for the patients of other physicians; at my entrance into any home to say, "May the peace of God

---

[20] Quoted by Dunn, 113.

[21] Quoted in *Stories of Prayer for a Healthy Soul*, compiled by Christine Anderson (Grand Rapids: Zondervan, 2000) 17.

abide here"; after hearing a sermon to pray for a blessing on God's truth and upon the messenger; upon the sight of a beautiful person to bless God...upon the sight of a deformed person to pray God to give them wholeness.[22]

Jesus said, "If you love Me, feed My sheep" (see John 21:17). The capacity to feed others is directly traceable to our love relationship with Jesus. If we become caught up in the work of the Lord, it will be too weighty, too crushing. The only way to do the work of the Lord is to worship our way into that work. We cannot worship our work; we must worship the Lord of the work.

One pastor confided in me that he feared that prayer would take over his church. I understood his concern for balance. He explained to me that there was so much more to a church than prayer. Without realizing it, he saw prayer as just another program and activity. I was secretly hoping that prayer would take over his church. Only through prayer can we wake up sensitivity to the Spirit realm, to the depth of the darkness with which we wrestle, and the glorious nature of the light. Prayer will deepen our compassion for the lost and open their eyes for salvation. Prayer will compel us toward a compassion for the lost, and embolden us with a witness.

William Law says, "There is nothing that makes us love someone so much as praying for them."[23] It

---

[22] Quoted by Duewel, *Touch the World Through Prayer,* 30-1.

[23] Bill Thrasher, *A Journey to Victorious Praying* (Chicago: Moody, 2003) 41.

is not less prayer that we need, it is more prayer. It is prayer until our hearts are on fire and our tongues cannot be quieted; prayer until we are exploding with the very real sense of God's presence. Andrew Murray declared, "The evangelization of the world depends first of all upon a revival of prayer. Deeper than the need for men—aye, deep down at the bottom of our spiritless life, is the need for the forgotten secret of prevailing, worldwide prayer."[24]

E.M. Bounds states:

> The more praying there is in the world, the better the world will be, the mightier the forces against evil everywhere. Prayer, in one phase of its operation, is a disinfectant and a preventative. It purifies the air; it destroys the contagion of evil. Prayer is no fitful, short-lived thing. It is no voice crying unheard and unheeded in the silence. It is a voice which goes into God's ear, and it lives as long as God's ear is open to holy pleas, as long as God's heart is alive to holy things. God shapes the world by prayer. Prayers are deathless. The lips that uttered them may be closed in death, the heart that felt them may have ceased to beat, but the prayers live before God, and God's heart is set on them and prayers outlive the lives of those who uttered them; they outlive a generation, outlive an age, outlive a world. That man is the most immortal who has done the most and the best praying. They are God's heroes, God's saints, God's servants, God's vice-regents. A man can pray better because of

---

[24] *http://www.liftupusa.com/pquotes.htm* (prayer quotes compiled by Miles Bennett).

the prayers of the past; a man can live holier because of the prayers of the past. The man of many and acceptable prayers has done the truest and greatest service to the incoming generation. The prayers of God's saints strengthen the unborn generation against the desolating waves of sin and evil.[25]

The lives of two brothers stand in stark contrast to one another. Here is their story:

Two hundred years ago, two Scottish brothers were launched from the same home. John wanted to make his mark on the world, make money and become wealthy. And he did. He has a brief mention in *Encyclopedia Britannica*. David set out to serve others, almost anonymously. Unlike his brother, he was not motivated to acquire wealth or fame. He resolved to place no value on any material thing he possessed unless he could define its purpose in relationship to the kingdom of God. He disappeared into the heart of uncharted territory and was unheard of for years. The first to penetrate an uncharted continent and see its extraordinary beauty, he was both explorer and holy man. He gave of himself—as a doctor, cartographer, diplomat, sociologist, peacemaker and missionary. At one time, the world seemed to hold its breath until it knew he was alive again. His obscurity seemed to guarantee his fame. The whole of Western civilization was gripped with his selfless devotion. On his last evening on the earth, he knelt in prayer by his cot. Looking in on him several times in

[25] E.M. Bounds, *The Best of E.M. Bounds* (Grand Rapids: Baker, 1981) 75.

the night, his assistants had assumed that he continued in prayer. He was discovered dead the next morning, and nations wept. His funeral procession covered 1,000 miles and lasted 11 months. There has never been another like it in history. His body was carried from Africa's interior to the coast of the Indian Ocean to be shipped home to England, as a yearlong tribute to his life. He is buried at Westminster Abbey. The inscription on his tombstone reads, "For 30 years his life was spent in an unwearied effort to evangelize."

On his 59th birthday, his diary records the entry: "My Jesus, my King, my Life, my All; I again dedicate my whole self to Thee." On the flyleaf of his Bible, he had written this prayer: "Lord, send me anywhere, only go with me. Lord, lay any burden on me, only sustain me. Lord, sever any ties except those ties that bind me to Thee and to Thy gospel."

In death, he still lives. In obscurity, he secured notoriety. In service, he came to command the respect of the world. In humility, he was exalted. In owning nothing, he seemed to own a whole continent, perhaps the whole world. Africa is forever grateful for his service, the service of David Livingstone. His brother, John? Check the older editions of *Encyclopedia Britannica*, and you will find him listed as . . . "the brother of David Livingstone"![26]

---

[26] McLellan, 219.

Conclusion

George Mueller ran his great benevolence endeavor on prayer. His 93-year life is loaded with one prayer miracle after another. The children would be called to an empty table with no bread in the orphanage, and Mueller would be on his knees interceding. Someone would show up with milk, bread or some other staple for the table. The children never went hungry. He cared for more than 10,000 children in five immense orphanages. And he raised more than $5 million through prayer. Mueller gave away 2 million Scriptures or Scripture portions. His publishing operation printed millions of tracts, books and Bibles for missionary-evangelism work. He sent $1 million to missions—an extraordinary sum in the 1800s. He pastored a church of 1,200. He wrote an average of 3,000 letters a year, most with his own hand. He led mission tours after his 71st birthday to 45 nations. It was his passion that inspired J. Hudson Taylor to found the China Inland Mission.

Many people think the social ministry of Mueller was the heart of his work. It wasn't. He was a man of prayer, a missionary, a father to orphans. But his passion was prayer. He would say, "I have made it a rule never to begin work until I have had a good season with God and His Word." He believed that one hour of prayer and four hours of work was more productive than five hours of work. He prayed with an open Bible. He read, then reflected. He read more, and meditated. He kept reading until something in the Scripture exploded in his heart and overflowed. He walked in the life of that truth all day. His primary and most important work was to make his "soul happy in the Lord" every day. He called it "soul nourishment."

Mueller would say later that he founded the orphanage not merely for humanitarian reasons, though that would have been noble. Rather, he wanted to demonstrate to the world that God was a prayer-answering God—a God who cared. He watched believers live vibrant lives of faith, grow old and become fearful, wondering if God would forsake them in their sunset years. He saw youth compromise their standards to prosper in the world, doubting that they could be successful and faithful too. Obsessed with success, they destroyed themselves operating with ravished souls and little peace. They are fractured families with more than others and simultaneously less.

Mueller wanted to demonstrate by prayer that God would more than care for His own if we would but trust Him. He determined to make his financial needs known only to God. He believed that God was so good, that prayer was so powerful that God could and would not only take care of him, but He would bless thousands of children as well. Mueller documented more than 50,000 answers to prayer.

His purpose was to demonstrate the character of God.[1] He is a good God. Those who come to Him must believe that He is a rewarder!

[1] A.T. Pierson, *George Mueller of Bristol* (New York: Revell, 1905) 112.

MINISTRY RESOURCES
by P. Douglas Small

Transforming Your Church Into a House of Prayer - Book

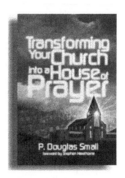

Prayer that is worshipful at its center and missional at its edge. You'll gain insights into a simple theology of prayer. You'll see how to structure your leadership team. You'll find a four-dimensional model for your prayer process. Ideas for your prayer room or prayer center will take new shape. Have a lot of people who are visual learners? There is an 8-session DVD series that serves as a companion to the book! The resource CD with this set has a PowerPoint presentation, companion notes, and more than 20 printable resource documents. The DVD series and book can be purchased separately or together! To get the most out of your experience, buy a case of books for your prayer leaders. Have them read a chapter and watch the video. Then discuss it together. Price: **$17.99**

Heaven Is a Courtroom - CD Set

Six messages recorded live at Central Church of God (Charlotte, NC) by P. Douglas Small. Topics include: Three Aspects of Prayer, Filing Your Petition, Pleading Your Case, Integrity, Building Your Case, and Breakthrough (Intensity in Prayer).
Price: **$30.00**

The Anointing Ministry of Jesus - CD Set

Wherever Jesus went the power of God flowed out of Him. And His promise was clear: "Greater things shall you do ... these signs shall follow them that believe in My name!" Are there any insights that could help us learn to be more available, more yielded, more of a vessel of the Holy Spirit to allow the work of Christ to be done through us? It is not technique! It is a heart thing. And yet, there are some principles worth gleaning as we look at the way the anointing flowed in the ministry of Jesus. Price: **$25.00**

Dreams, Destiny and Discipline - CD Set

Every person has a personal destiny! God has a plan for your life! Like Joseph, there are God-given dreams afforded to each of us. However, the manner in which those dreams come to pass are often in ways that confound, confuse, and cause us to lose our way. Who could have ever charted the route by which God fulfilled the dreams of Joseph? Written off as dead, accused of immorality, imprisoned, and forgotten—God raised him up for His glory. Your life also has a purpose! In two tapes, Doug lays out principles for seeing your way through the world's fog and finding fulfillment by discovering yourself in the will and work of the Lord! Price: **$15.00**

Exploring Islam in the Light of Christianity - CD Set

Five dynamic messages recorded live at Central Church of God (Charlotte, NC) by P. Douglas Small. Topics include: A Spiritual Attack on America; Comparison of the Koran to the Word of God; The Muslim Faith in the Light of the Apostles' Creed; Who Is Mohammed?; Who is Jesus? Price: **$35.00**

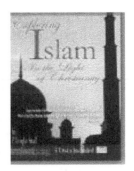

The 7 Spiritual Gifts of Romans - CD Set

An incredible series! The motivational gifts in Romans 12 are the forgotten spiritual gifts. Everybody has them! Everyone! These native gifts are to be dedicated to God, "Present your bodies as living sacrifices!" Why? God designed these gifts as delivery systems for his grace. In fact, the real gift is never for example, just the principles. Likewise, the gift is not in the giving of the giver, it is God's grace in the act of giving itself. But more so, these motivational gifts have limits. Mercy can love, but mercy cannot heal. These gifts will only take us so far—then mercy hits a wall, and leadership is puzzled, and giving is out of resources. That is when the motivational gifts interface with the manifestation gifts of Corinthians 12. Standing at the bedside of a sick loved one, mercy gives way to the gift of healing. Standing at a crossroads, leadership is endowed with the gift of wisdom. Out of resources, giving is given a miracle provision.
Price **$30.00**

The Blood Covenant

The Blood Covenant is the oldest covenant known to man other than Marriage! The Blood Covenant is at the heart of the Christian Communion experience, yet the average believer knows almost nothing about it! This CD set will cover the importance and the strength that the Blood Covenant which we hold with Jesus Christ really is! Price: **$15.00**

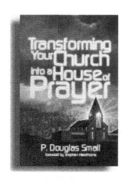

Transforming Your Church Into a House of Prayer - DVD Set

This DVD set includes: Extensive Student Training Notes, Converted PowerPoint Presentations, and more than 20 resource documents! The session titles are as follows: Session 1-Theology of Prayer; Session 2-Philosophy of Prayer; Session 3-The Prayer Center; Session 4-Understanding Mission, Vision and Values; Session 5-Building a Prayer Leadership Team for Impact!; Session 6-The Discovery Process. Price: **$59.99**

Order Online at
www.projectpray.org